# Gloryous Dance Affair

# Gloryous Dance Affair

Black and white

Best Wishes
Glorya Kaufman

*Glorya Kaufman and Deborah Schwartz*

ISBN: 1537554093
ISBN 13: 9781537554099

**To my husband, Donald Bruce Kaufman, without whose vision and innovative spirit my life and my ability to help others would not have been possible**

# Contents

# Foreword

*Gloryous Dance Affair* is an inspirational and emotional roller coaster of a journey that chronicles the life of one of America's most impressive and radiant women, Glorya Kaufman. This emotional page-turner, filled with guts, humor, and tears, is a must-read for anyone seeking inspiration or courage to move forward despite seemingly insurmountable odds.

Finding courage and strength from within, reinventing herself, and discovering the voice she lacked until her husband's untimely death, Glorya was not content to just move forward. Once the sunlight of renewed life and hope hit her face, there was no stopping this brand-new Glorya Kaufman. She was ready to take on whomever and whatever was necessary to follow her dream.

Glorya grew up in a modest family in Detroit. Her parents, both hard workers who valued their Jewish heritage, set the stage and modeled for her the key to life that they held dear: helping those less fortunate. With their guidance, her dream took form.

Originally, her dream of founding an orphanage began with saving pennies in the tzedakah box her mother provided for the family. Her modest habit of putting pennies into this little blue box led to her multimillion-dollar philanthropic work for the disadvantaged and her contributions to the rescue of dance as an art form, which earned her the title "Duchess of Dance."

I met Glorya in 1982 when I began dating my wife, Deborah. Our first date was horseback riding at the Kaufmans' beautiful ranch home in Brentwood. The Glorya I knew then was Don Kaufman's wife, and Gayl, Stacie, Curtis, and Laura Kaufman's mother, and that was the extent of it.

This beautiful ranch and beautiful family were soon to be shattered by Don's tragic death, which catapulted everyone in the family into a different direction. After losing her husband of twenty-eight years, Glorya was brave enough to take a long, hard, critical look at herself. For anyone, this is a daunting task at best, but she decided that she wanted to change herself before she went on to decide how she wanted to help others. As they say: "Put your own oxygen mask on first." That's what Glorya did. She helped herself and became ready for charitable work.

In addition to her multiple gifts for helping children and the disadvantaged, her generous gifts to support the art of dance through her foundation are groundbreaking. In collaboration with the University of Southern California, Glorya's vision of a world-class dance school on the West Coast is no longer a dream; it is a reality. The Glorya Kaufman I knew in 1982 was someone's mother and someone's wife. The Glorya Kaufman I know now is classy, fun-loving, smart, hardworking, generous, loving, kind, and most of all, unwavering in her quest to make the world a better place for children and adults. Whether it be one person at a time, or one community at a time, whether she is creating an international dance school with USC or providing eye care for preschool children at the Jules Stein Clinic, Glorya never quits.

Take to dreaming big, take risks—and never take no for an answer. Glorya doesn't. Read on and explore her journey in *Gloryous Dance Affair.*

*Douglas Schwartz*

Douglas Schwartz is a writer and producer of the television series *Baywatch*, and he is the producer of the soon-to-be-released major motion picture *Baywatch.*

# Preface

> I've always believed that there was a purpose for my life, and that I had to seek that purpose, and that if I discovered that purpose, then I believed that I would be successful in what I was doing.
>
> —Coretta Scott King

I TREASURE THE MULTIMEDIA PAINTING by Colombian artist Orlando that hangs in my office. This painting provides me with a daily reminder of how far I have come in becoming my own person, managing my own life, and, most important, being seen and heard on my own terms. When I was a child, children were often raised to be seen and not heard, and I was no exception.

A friend of mine had asked me to go with him to pick out some artwork for his apartment, which I was more than happy to do. I spotted a marionette painting and suggested he buy it for himself. He said, "Glorya, you can't take your eyes off of it. I think you should buy it for yourself."

He was right, and I bought it on the spot.

I asked the gallery to reframe the painting, replacing the black frame with a soft ivory one with gold trim. The new frame allowed me to see something I had not seen before: very fine black strings attached to the puppet's arms and legs. The reason I did not see the strings is that the background of the painting is gold and copper leaf; the strings all but disappear when one first looks at it. After studying it, I realized it was a portrait of me: a sleeping puppet.

When my husband, Don, was killed in a bi-wing airplane accident, I was forced by circumstance to become an independent person for the first time in my life. I had to learn to be strong. Throughout my life, I had had strong-willed people guiding me. First my mother and later my husband took over, pulling my strings by making decisions for me, who was just like the marionette in the painting. I thus had to cut the strings and learn to dance to my own tune.

Two things would prove to be my saving grace and help me find my purpose after Don's death: the sustaining memory of my father's love, and dancing. I want to share with others the beauty of dance so that they can experience the joy and lightness of being that I felt as I danced about on my father's toes. While the tragedy of losing Don is always with me, the journey onward has truly been a *Gloryous Dance Affair.*

Regarding the structure of this book, I have organized this memoir into four sections: Early Life, Marriage, Starting Again, and Philanthropy, with an Interlude in the middle. The narrative in the early chapters is strictly my own, but beginning with my years in California, I have incorporated the words of friends and colleagues who have shared this journey. Each of them brings a unique and meaningful perspective to my story, and I am very grateful for their contributions.

Glorya Kaufman, 2016

**Marionette painting**

PART 1

# Early Life

# Beginnings

I HAD A WONDERFUL FATHER who loved to dance. He would let me stand barefoot on the top of his shoes so we could dance to the tunes on the radio. He died two years after my husband, and I was able to tell him that, but for his love, I do not believe I could have survived the difficulty of becoming a young widow. His memory still sustains me today.

My parents were of Eastern European descent, and they both came, independently, from Toronto to Detroit. They were the poster couple for opposites attracting.

My father was loving, kind, and nonjudgmental. By contrast, my mother was brutally honest, almost to a fault. As the oldest of ten children, my mother had to quit school to help raise her siblings. She went to work in a sewing factory when she was fourteen years old. Thus, Mother became a skilled perfectionist in every task imaginable in a household, with the exception of giving and receiving love and affection. In photographs of me with my mother when I was a child, she rarely had an affectionate arm around me. In contrast, I have my arms wrapped around her as if I am an accessory hanging on for dear life.

Mother always had delicious food for guests to munch on when they came for a visit. I suspect they all overlooked my mother's lack of any sense of humor because my father was so easygoing and fun to be around. My dad would pitch baseball at the local school on Saturdays. A lot of the boys loved to play or watch the games, and they all called my dad "Pinky." At break time, Dad would buy all the kids a soda pop. My dad was a sucker for kids and loved being around them. My childhood dream was to run a home for orphaned children. I just wanted to take care of them. I am sure I learned this love for children from reading *Little Orphan Annie*. In my later years, when I began to date, my suitors would all look forward to visiting with my dad. He was their local hero.

Mother was president of seven Jewish organizations that helped the homeless, hungry, or people in need of medication. Although I was not the beneficiary of her selfless efforts, my mother's commitment to helping others made a huge and lasting impression on me.

During my younger years, my dad held down several jobs at a time. My mother needed a great deal of medical care, and the bills were high. I remember frequent surgeries and hospitalizations. Despite her medical history, she lived well into her nineties. Dad would often borrow money from the bank to pay the bills on time, making sure that he would have only one loan to pay, with interest. He was a proud and honest man, and he never wanted others, except the bank charging interest, to have to wait for money that he owed them.

We lived in an apartment for my entire childhood. One hot, humid summer day, when I was eighteen months old, I began to shiver while playing in a plastic pool with the children next door. Thinking that I was shivering because I was cold, my mother put me into a very warm bathtub, which caused convulsions, sending me into shock. Not long after, she noticed that my eyes were not aligned. I was left with a condition known as strabismus, an inability of the eyes to align themselves correctly.

I was a cross-eyed, tiny wisp of a thing with a heart murmur. And to top it off, my hair was silky and straight instead of lustrous like my mother's and my sister Edythe's hair.

I spent the next eight years being teased and made fun of by other children. When I got tired, while one eye remained focused, I could feel the other eye lose control and move toward my nose. I became very self-conscious because I had no control over this. I was extremely aware that I looked odd. When the kids would tease me, calling me "cross eyes," or "four eyes," it hurt terribly, adding to my already low self-esteem. I was even more self-conscious around boys than girls, but in spite of all the teasing and my constant state of embarrassment, I always had girlfriends.

My vision impairment made reading a slow and tedious process at best. Even though my great hearing compensated for my poor vision, I would often strain so hard to see that I ended up with excruciating headaches. Nevertheless, I enjoyed school and managed to do well. It helped that I had an artistic sensibility, particularly when it came to balance and symmetry. I had a knack for placing a picture in just the right location to show it off, or for placing a vase or figurine where it would best enhance the space. Even as a child, I was bothered when objects were not placed aesthetically. To this day, it is very annoying to me to see things out of balance in a room.

When I was about seven, I decided to change the spelling of my name from "Gloria" to "Glorya" because I felt the *L* and the *Y* balanced each other in a symmetrical way. In keeping with the Jewish tradition of naming a child after a special, deceased loved one, I was named after Gittel Nacoma, my father's Romanian grandmother. My father never knew her, because his parents left Romania and moved to Canada when he was an infant. But he was told, and he then told me, that she was a brilliant and beautiful woman. My parents used her initials, naming me Gloria Naomi.

My artistic flair contributed to a boost in my confidence, and I was very proud when one of my teachers selected my drawings for display in the showcase in the McCulloch Elementary School hallway. I was only about six at the time, but I will never forget that feeling of pride. Nor will I ever forget my first-grade teacher, Miss Temple. She had a lovely smile and blond hair that she wore in a twist at the back of her head. Looking back now, I know she gave me special attention because she knew I needed it. That was part of her beauty. She was a great boon to my confidence, and I was so very proud when she assigned me the job of erasing the blackboard at the end of the day. Some might have seen it as a chore, but I saw it as a privilege and an honor, which I know is how she meant it to be. That year, as a Christmas present, Miss Temple gave me a silver bracelet with a turquoise stone in the center. I felt so special that I practically never took that bracelet off. I was extremely upset to look down one day and see that the stone had fallen out of the setting. I finally decided that it was still beautiful and if you didn't know the stone was there to begin with, you wouldn't miss it. I wore that bracelet for years because it reminded me of Miss Temple and her kindness. I wish she knew how much she helped me and that I never forgot her. After many moves, I finally lost the bracelet, but I have never forgotten Miss Temple, and I have kept her safe in my heart forever.

My sister Edythe enjoyed a multitude of lessons in tap, ballet, speech, piano, singing, art, and whatever else would guide her toward my mother's dream of making Edythe a movie star. At that time, I worshipped my sister. To me, while we were growing up, she was already a star. Sometimes I was allowed to go inside and watch Edythe's dance lessons with the dance instructor, Mr. Cusetta, and I was in awe. I was transfixed by the beauty, symmetry, and elegance of dance. I dreamed of being in his class one day and having him teach me all those beautiful dances. But that never happened. My only extracurricular activity was going to see Dr. Ralph Pino in downtown Detroit to have lessons in eye-strengthening. The exercises involved a machine that tracked my eyes while I watched images of a moving ball or a bird flying into a cage. Following this movement with my eyes was supposed to strengthen my eye muscles. Dr. Pino would mark my progress, but little was gained compared to what surgery could accomplish. These practices are no longer used today, according to Dr. Steven Schwartz of the Jules Stein Eye Clinic. In fact, they may even be harmful.

Physical beauty meant a great deal to my mother. In a quest to make my hair curly, she gave me a Toni Home Permanent. The permanent solution smelled, and the strong vapors stung my eyes. It didn't make my hair curly and beautiful. After all the torture of the smell and the tight curlers, it just made my hair fuzzy.

While Edythe was busy with her extracurricular activities, mine were curtailed because of my slight heart murmur. I was treated as an invalid, which furthered the isolation I felt as a child. While I rested on a cot at school, I listened to the other children as they laughed, played, and participated in sports—and I dreamed of being able to join them.

Even though my older sister had the benefit of my mother's ambitions, both Edythe and I suffered from our mother's physical abuse. Mother was a hot-tempered disciplinarian, and her perfectionism extended to my sister and me. Times were different when I was growing up. Child Protective Services did not yet exist, shockingly; it was not founded until 1974, and there were very few child welfare laws. The phrase "spare the rod, spoil the child" was certainly still in vogue, and the rod was something my mother prescribed on more occasions than I care to remember. This kind of cruelty at my mother's hand was painful to endure and painful to acknowledge, and it remains extremely painful to put into words, especially in print. We often felt the sting of whippings with one of my father's belts. Our backsides stung for days, and I would look in the mirror at the red welt on my fanny, feeling perplexed as to what could make my mother so angry. This was just another hit to my self-esteem and a factor in the shame I felt, but I grew to understand that it was frustration with her own life that drove her to abuse us. On more than one occasion, Edythe and I would take the belt she had whipped us with and toss it into the incinerator down the hall from our apartment. My poor father couldn't figure out why his belts were disappearing. When we would hear him question my mother about them, we made ourselves scarce in a hurry.

Thank God for my father's love and support. He encouraged me every step of the way. In later years, my dad told me that his nickname for me was "Bubbles" because I was such a happy, giggling child. I always felt Dad's love. My aunts, uncles, and cousins in Detroit and Toronto also made me feel loved and cared for. They made a special effort to boost my self-esteem because they were witnesses to my mother's extreme favoring of Edythe and exclusion of me. Buoyed by my father, my relatives, and special teachers like Miss Temple, I managed to stay afloat emotionally. I never felt entitled to the opportunities bestowed on Edythe, and it wasn't until I had my eye surgery that I even felt worthy. Edythe felt nothing but entitlement through her entire life, which was detrimental to her growth as an adult.

The city of Detroit did not recover economically from the Depression until World War II, when the factories began producing tanks and warplanes and the city became known as "the arsenal of democracy." It was around this time that my father became the production manager for *Automotive News*, a newspaper that specialized in the newest gadgets and innovative designs for cars, that was distributed throughout the United States. As my father started doing better financially, he would buy my mother beautiful gifts. Since she could never get away from the austerity of the Depression years and allow enjoyment into her life, she would return the gifts and keep the money. Even as a child, I knew that my mother was not only unhappy but incapable of finding happiness. When my mother passed away in her nineties, I felt deeply saddened by the realization that she never really enjoyed life and that she never felt recognized for all she did for her family and her organizations. If only she could have grasped that the validation she needed had to come from within. It is a great sadness of mine that I could never help my mother, or that she would never have allowed me to help. It haunts me that I have few memories of my mother laughing.

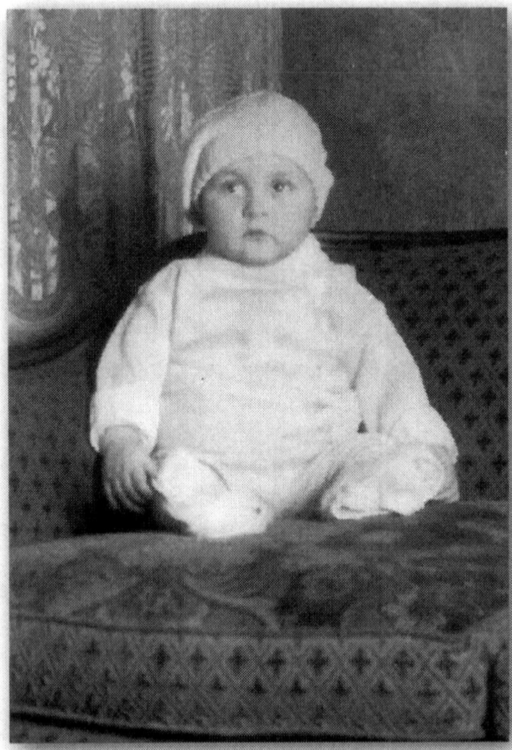

**Baby Glorya**

**Glorya and her older sister, Edythe**

**Glorya in a pink silk dress made by her mother, Eva**

# The Eyes Have It

THERE ARE SO MANY CRUEL things that go on in the world today, especially where children are concerned. Whenever I see a movie or a television show in which a child is teased or taunted, I instantly recall my feelings of being bullied because of my crossed eyes. This is one reason why I strive to do whatever I can to better the lives of children through my philanthropic endeavors. I am thrilled to see the many organizations and famous personalities speaking out against bullying. It is important to educate children in school about the extreme damage caused by bullying and to send a clear message that this is unacceptable behavior that will not be tolerated. It is equally important to educate parents.

In those days we did not have the skills or education necessary to fight against bullying. The taunts were so emotionally painful for me that I became very depressed and wouldn't eat. Because I was already so thin that a stiff breeze could knock me off balance, my lack of appetite was of great concern to my parents.

I was ten years old when my parents realized they needed to do something more about my eyes. They had put off the decision due to my general frailty and slight heart murmur, but now the time had come for me to have surgery. I later learned that the best time for surgery is when the condition first occurs and before the brain has a chance to compensate, impairing vision forever. Despite my history with strabismus, Dr. Pino was confident that the surgery would help me. I already knew him from my many visits for eye strengthening. He was a kind and gentle man who could gain my confidence and boost my spirits at the same time. He told me my eyes were beautiful, and I believed him. Dr. Pino instilled in me the notion that I was worthy of admiration.

The surgery was performed during my summer vacation, which caused me even more depression. While all the other kids were out playing and enjoying their summer, I was having surgery. I awoke from the surgery with thick bandages on my eyes, and needless to say, it was frightening. Trying to move my eyes under the bandages was painful. I must have been in a private room at the hospital, because I don't remember hearing anyone talking, except for the nurses and doctors who were scurrying about. Even though my parents came to visit me every day, I still felt alone and scared. I was confined to bed, and the nurses would give me sponge baths. Every night as I lay alone in my bed, listening to the various hospital noises, I prayed that when all was healed I would look normal. I worried about so many scenarios that a child my age should not have been worrying about. My head buzzed with negative thoughts: *What if the doctor could not fix my eyes? What if I had to go through this again? Would I ever be able to read? Would my friends still like me if I were blind? Would people feel sorry for me?* I surely didn't want pity. I wanted one very simple thing: to be normal.

After I had spent ten long and difficult days confined to my bed in the hospital, it was time for the bandages to be removed. The nurse removing the bandages was very gentle with me. I have no idea what she looked like because I could not see, but I will never forget her comforting voice. I think it was then that I began to develop a keen sense of hearing and the ability to really listen to a voice and recognize it instantly when I heard it next.[1] The nurse's voice soothed me while she worked on cleaning up my eyes. They had crusted over from blood and residue, and she took her time, cleaning them slowly, ever so careful to be gentle and cause me the least discomfort possible. When I was finally able to open my eyes, they hurt terribly. Part of it was the bright light, as my eyes had been shut for ten days. But all I could register was the pain, and it lasted for weeks. I was so hoping to look normal, just normal. But when I looked in the mirror and saw that the whites of my eyes were red I was

1 My acute hearing would be a compensatory tool throughout my childhood and adolescence. In school I became an aural learner as excessive reading could be painful.

not only disappointed, I was terrified. The redness eventually faded, and the surgery did result in my eyes aligning correctly, but my vision was impaired. I saw a halo around everything I looked at, especially when reading. The halo would blend the letters and words together, making them indistinguishable. Because of this, I still had to wear thick glasses. The frames were large and heavy on my tiny face—but I was no longer cross-eyed! For the first time in my life the phrase "cross-eyed" no longer defined me. I felt as if I had been transformed into a normal child.

I would continue to struggle with vision problems throughout my life. As a teenager, I would just take my glasses off and rely on my hearing to navigate. When I was a young adult and contact lenses hit the market, the ability to shed the glasses and wear the contacts was a huge blessing for me. This alone transformed me from a shy girl into a confident young woman. Interestingly, it wouldn't be until 2007 when Dr. Kevin Miller from UCLA performed cataract surgery on me that I would finally have twenty-twenty vision.

I am so thankful that my eyesight was preserved. I am equally thankful that surgery techniques have improved so greatly that children who are afflicted with strabismus no longer need suffer through a painful surgery. I was relieved to learn that the procedure that is now performed to correct strabismus is not an invasive surgery. Happily, medicine has improved greatly, and specialists are now able to perform the surgery as soon as the condition is diagnosed. It can be performed on an outpatient basis with no blood, no bandages, and a 95 percent success rate. This resonates with me so profoundly that I am creating two funds with two large hospitals to assist families who cannot afford the surgery for their children. It delights me to know that many children will not have to suffer the humiliation and pain that I experienced. If what I had to endure ends up sparing other children from being set on that path, then my experience was not in vain. So many children can grow up with better vision if their problems are addressed when they are young. And that will give me great solace. It's not the orphanage I had dreamed of building—but it's a start.

One afternoon I was talking with my friend, the late Dr. Leonard Apt. Leonard was professor emeritus in the field of pediatric ophthalmology at the

Jules Stein Eye Institute, and he had received many prestigious awards for his innovative work. He made a unique scientific contribution to the field of pediatric ophthalmology as developer of antiseptic eye drops that substantially reduce the incidence of blindness.

After the meeting, I asked Leonard about the earliest and most effective age to check children's eyes. He told me that the best time to find an eye problem in children is between three and five but that children's eye problems were usually not detected until they were in the second or third grade. By that time several things have occurred. The children are already behind in class because they cannot see. This makes them feel stupid and also hinders their learning. The Jules Stein Institute had already established a mobile unit that traveled from school to school; however, it was for older children. I told Leonard that I would fund a project if he would convince the Jules Stein Institute to have retired doctors volunteer to check the children at preschool facilities. With all his charm, he persuaded them to allow a mobile preschool unit to visit nurseries and preschools and have the children's eyes examined. The first examination was accomplished at the Donald Bruce Kaufman Brentwood Branch Library. There were more than seventy children that came for eye exams. The project was launched and continued for twelve or thirteen years.

Then a miracle happened. Jules Stein received a grant of $4 million for mobile-unit examinations at preschools. I was told that this would mean that ninety thousand children would receive examinations within the next five years. I was thrilled when I read the announcement in the Jules Stein newspaper. My only sadness was that dear Dr. Leonard Apt had passed, and we could not share this wonderful moment together.

Since UCLA would only provide examinations, parents were left to find doctors for treatment or glasses. I opened an eye clinic at the Venice Free Clinic in Santa Monica. This enabled the children to receive further care, free eyeglasses, and, if needed, further treatment at Los Angeles Children's Hospital.

I decided to have USC sell my apartment in Paris on Avenue Montaigne and use the funds from the sale to establish a department at the Roski Eye Institute to provide free surgery to children suffering from strabismus.

I am extremely happy and proud of my collaboration with Dr. Leonard Apt of the Jules Stein Clinic. I am blessed to be able to make a difference to children with vision issues.

**Glorya and Dr. Leonard Apt holding the Jules Stein preschool eye-exam book**

# Teenage Dream Years

*When we are children we seldom think of the future. This innocence leaves us free to enjoy ourselves as few adults can. The day we fret about the future is the day we leave our childhood behind.*

—PATRICK ROTHFUSS, *THE NAME OF THE WIND*

AS I REFLECT ON MY teen years, I remember my sense of innocence, my lack of real concerns or worries about the future. With my vision problems under control during my teen years, I lived and loved every day, and I never remember any of my crowd getting into any trouble. As puberty set in, I started to become a young woman. Instead of looking in the mirror and crying because I was so ugly, I began to like the girl smiling back at me. I also quit worshipping my sister after an episode involving an aqua suit.

I spent many Friday and Saturday nights babysitting to save up money for a beautiful aqua suit made of gabardine. I loved it the moment I saw it, and I bought it to wear for my junior-high-school graduation. I was so proud of saving the money to buy it and having such a beautiful suit to wear. Edythe decided to wear my suit on a date without telling me. She accidentally burned a huge hole in the beautiful suit while pressing it. I discovered this when I went to wear it for the second time. She had intentionally neglected to tell me. Because she always got her way, there were no ramifications for Edythe from either of my parents. For me, it was their failure to rebuke Edythe more than the loss of the suit that stung.

Over time I quit letting Edythe walk all over me. As I became more assertive, I gained confidence in myself.

Dad always chauffeured me to and from the AZA Jewish dances. I had become very accomplished at identifying voices when I wasn't wearing my glasses so I could recognize my friends calling to me from across the room. I always greeted people with enthusiasm. If someone didn't speak, it would take me a few seconds to recognize them, and I didn't want to risk not greeting a friend warmly. So I greeted everyone that way—with great enthusiasm! I still do.

I had many girlfriends. Whenever one of us had a date, we would pool our clothes to come up with the perfect outfit. We had fun joking, giggling, and dancing. I found that if I could follow a young man on the dance floor, he was more than happy to dance with me. Dancing instilled confidence in me. In those days the idea of having sex with these young men was not even an option in my circle of friends. Just the thought of shaming our parents kept us under control.

When I was fifteen, my girlfriends and I started a club called "The Aedorns." We had white hats with monograms that we designed with the initials *AE*, with the *E* on a slight slant. Every Friday evening, we would hold a dance at the home of one of the members whose house had a recreation room, and we'd invite a different boys' club each time. None of us took formal dancing lessons. We just taught ourselves the new popular dances and perfected the old favorites: the cha-cha, rumba, jitterbug, samba, and mambo. We left no dance undanced! We would put records on the Victrola and dance for hours until a parent would tell us that it was time to call it a night. The confidence that dancing gave me changed my personality. As my shyness melted away, an exuberance replaced it. Dance truly changed the quality of my life.

I spent many nights dancing in Detroit's small nightclubs. They were called "black and tan" clubs because most of the musicians were black. Since I was not twenty-one, the legal age for drinking, I had to borrow an ID from an older cousin or friend. But it wasn't to drink. It was just to get into the club to dance! Once I hit the dance floor, I never wanted to sit down. Dancing was my oxygen. It made me feel alive and vibrant. If my date did not prove to be a good dancer, that was it. No second chance—or second date. The music, South American and full of melody and rhythm, won me many bottles of champagne, the first prize in the dance contests. Even though they only drank on special occasions, I would bring the champagne home to my parents after dancing the night away. It was a wonderful time, an innocent time.

My father, who was now working for *Automotive News*, also belonged to the Printers Union. Unbeknown to me, he had sent my picture to the office and entered me in a Labor Day beauty contest. I was reluctant, but to please my father and not let him down, I went to the interview. I had only been to beauty pageants as an observer, when Edythe was entered by my mother. As I sat waiting my turn, I looked around the room at all the beautiful girls. I felt so out of my league. I didn't have a chance and just wanted to get out of there as quickly as possible to avoid any further embarrassment. I left immediately after my interview, hoping to put this all behind me. The next day I received a phone call from a nice gentleman wanting to know why I had disappeared after the interview. I told him the truth—that I had left because I didn't think I had a chance. He said, "Well, young lady, you were wrong. We selected you as the winner, but when we found you had already left, we went with our second choice."

Could I really rely on my ears to believe what I had just heard? I had won! The nice gentleman insisted that I still be a part of the festivities as a princess and ride down Woodward Avenue in the convertible with the queen. What fun it was to get all dressed up with my hair done special and ride in the Cadillac convertible, waving to the crowd. I know my father was so proud he was about to burst.

The aqua suit, Durfee Intermediate School

# Road Trips

WITHOUT FAIL, MY DAD TOOK the train to and from work every day. Then one day he came home driving a new Oldsmobile. Oh, how he loved that car. He never drove anything but an Oldsmobile for the rest of his life. Having this car changed our vacation life. One of the reasons our family had not purchased a house, as so many of our friends had, is that Dad loved road trips with the family. Instead of saving for a house, he spent his money on the car and taking the family on vacations. I have to admire that. It was a choice, but Dad chose to spend time with his family and make them happy. I could never fault him for that. Every year he used his bonus to take us all on an adventure. This is one of the things I ended up loving so much about Don. He had a lust for adventure, just as I did. And it all started with our road trips. I have such warm and delicious memories of sitting with my sister in the back seat with Dad at the wheel and Mother riding shotgun. Edythe and I had to get along because Dad wouldn't have tolerated anything less. Dad had a nice voice and would sing as we drove, but I think he was kind of disappointed that neither of his girls could sing. Whether we were off on a road trip to Florida, California, or a national park like Yosemite or the Grand Canyon, we had a wonderful time. It was great to see all the beautiful scenery as we traveled along in the beloved Oldsmobile, playing games in the car. My dad loved the family togetherness, and we all loved staying at the next fun motel or hotel.

One of my favorite trips took place every two years when we would all pile into the car to visit our relatives in Toronto, where both sets of grandparents lived. My dad's parents were quite elderly and didn't speak English, so communication was mostly hugs, smiles, and kisses. They had the most fabulous cherry tree in their backyard and most of my time was spent picking cherries. I just couldn't wait to see my cousins. The whole family would stay with my dad's sister, Auntie Pearl, and her husband, Luppa Silverstone. They had four children: Clara, Lillian, Phoebe, and Morton. They lived on Bloor Street, a major commercial thoroughfare, above Uncle Luppa's tailor shop. Uncle Luppa made men's clothes, and the woolen fabric was very heavy. One year he made me and my sister long black coats tailored to last for many seasons. When we wore them to and from school, they were so heavy that they weighed our shoulders down. But it was hard to hold those coats against Uncle Luppa. He loved us so much, and so did Auntie Pearl.

The first order of business upon arriving at the Silverstone home was to sit down at the kitchen table with Auntie Pearl and a huge cup of hot cocoa. We always looked forward to spending time with our cousins. Morton was my age, but the three girls were about fifteen years older than Edythe and me, and they treated us as if we were little dolls. Years later Morton told me that he had a crush on me when we were young. I was flattered. Morton loved playing the piano and actually wanted to pursue it as a career, but his parents convinced him to set his sights on a more practical path, so Morton became a dentist. He never really liked being a dentist and continued to play piano as a hobby. I thought it a shame, and it always made me sad that he was never able to try for his dream.

On one of our trips to Toronto, Edythe and I were to be bridesmaids at Phoebe's wedding. The day before the wedding I went to a community pool and sunbathed. I ended up with a horrific sunburn, and when I put on my beautiful lilac bridesmaid dress that my mother had made for the occasion, it was impossible to tell where the dress ended and my colorful sunburn began. I almost fainted before the ceremony but managed to get through it with grace. I would have felt terrible if I had disrupted my cousin's wedding.

What I really wanted to do more than anything else at that wedding was dance. I had a crush on a boy named Jerry Newton and he was supposed to come to the wedding. I was disappointed to hear from his parents that he had to stay home and take care of his younger brother. I went to the ladies' room, and when I returned, to my surprise, there was Jerry! A friend had stepped in to babysit his brother. I instantly became the happiest girl in the world. I was ecstatic that I was going to be able to dance with him.

Dancing and Jerry were my two favorite things. Jerry was my first love, and he belonged to a fraternity, which I just thought was so cool. He took me there to meet his Canadian fraternity brothers and introduced me as his special friend from the States. He was very handsome, and I must say he set my mind to dreaming. I really never had an official boyfriend in high school. I dated, and my boyfriends were mostly good dancers. Edythe, of course, did have a boyfriend in high school. It was almost too unbelievable to be true: Her boyfriend was Allen Weiss, the captain of the football team.

We loved visiting with the Silverstone family, but we would also have fun visiting my mother's parents, Sarah and Isaac Lepofsky. They lived just a few blocks from the corner grocery store. Grandpa Isaac was so proud of Edythe and me. He would take us to the corner for an orange Creamsicle, our favorite treat. We were his oldest grandchildren, and he wanted to show us off to anyone and everyone he could. It felt great to have him beam with pride over me.

I truly adored visiting my relatives and only wish we could have traveled to see them more often. Every time we saw them we had grown and changed so much that they were shocked. It was fun to see the looks on their faces when I blossomed and became a young woman. My cousins always remained close to me, and I was very touched when they all came to California for my father's (their Uncle Sam's) funeral. I had just lost Don two years and one week to the day before my father's death, and it was a very tough time for me.

# Stepping into the World

In the early fifties, Edythe left home and moved to California. I was coming into my own during high school and wanted to become a model!

I saved my money from whatever part-time jobs I had, and I took a John Robert Powers modeling class. At the time, Powers was the top modeling school, and there was a great deal that I enjoyed learning. The experience helped me tremendously. Over the course of many weeks, I learned how to walk properly, how to get in and out of a car gracefully, and many other confidence-enhancing techniques. Makeup application, hairstyling, exercise, and diet were also a part of the curriculum. We would also be taught how to "work it": walking the runway and modeling whatever outfit we wore. After graduating from Powers, I set out to model at fashion shows and luncheons after school and on weekends. I was required to wear heavy makeup, which I did not like doing, but I knew it was part of the job. I, of course, was very naïve and didn't really understand what the fashion world was all about.

The men who organized the fashion shows were the store owners or representatives of various clothing lines, and they all had one thing in common: They were often aggressive with the young girls. Though I very much enjoyed learning how to be a model and making extra money, I was definitely not a fan of the modeling scene. On the one hand, it was a real confidence booster for a girl like me who grew up thinking she wasn't very pretty. But it was also pretty grim. The people in the business made me very uncomfortable, and I ended up quitting. Still, it was a good experience, and the techniques I learned stuck with me forever.

While I was in high school I bought my first car, an Oldsmobile, which of course Dad had decided was the best car on the road. It was silver and certainly wouldn't have been described as a hot-looking car, but it was heavy and safe, and it was what Dad wanted me to drive. The luxury of having my own car gave me a great deal of independence. When my folks went on their winter holidays to Miami, I was able to get around, and they could relax and enjoy themselves with their friends. My mother's sister, Aunt Lill, knowing I was alone, would invite me over for dinner, and I would bring candy and flowers. She made the very best and most beautiful lemon pies I have ever eaten. Aunt Lill knew they were my favorite, and I don't believe I ever went to her home when there were not several fresh-baked lemon pies on display. Lemon pie is still my favorite dessert, but no one has ever been able to out-bake my Aunt Lill.

We were close with my mother's family and always shared the Jewish holidays. No matter who hosted the evening, everyone would pitch in and work together to create a fabulous dinner and great memories. It was great fun to visit my Uncle Morrie and Aunt Flo. Their two daughters, Edye and Beryl, loved to hear stories about the boys I was dating. I had a boyfriend named Seymour who was very handsome. He drove a Good Humor truck down their street and would give the girls free ice cream. I don't know which was the bigger treat, the free ice cream, or the handsome guy. Whichever it was, when the bells from the truck began to jingle, the girls made tracks.

Beside babysitting, my first job was selling chemistry sets at Sears and Roebuck. I was only fourteen, but between that and babysitting money, I was actually pretty flush. While I attended Durfee Junior High, I took a home-economics class that taught us how to place patterns on material, cut them out, and sew them together. I made many of my own outfits and liked to set myself apart from everyone else with my own style. I still do. I really enjoyed sewing and spent many Saturday afternoons at the fabric store selecting materials and patterns to design and make my own clothes.

Another one of my after-school and weekend jobs while I was in high school was as a receptionist in the dental office of Dr. Newmark. My job was to answer phones and greet patients. Saturday mornings always started out with Dr. Newmark telling the patients some jokes. They were funny to hear for the first few patients. But by the end of the day I had heard them twenty times, and I quit laughing. He would tell those afternoon patients that his assistant had no sense of humor.

I loved bike riding. At one point I had my eye on a beautiful two-toned bicycle. It was a rich blue and turquoise. I was very proud that I had earned every penny to pay for that bike, and I loved it as if it were a beloved pet. I would ride around the city with my friend Audrey Roberts, and we both enjoyed the feeling of independence and the freedom of bike riding. I later gave the bike to my cousin Rona.

But now all my hard-earned money was going to pay for my education, not clothes and not a bicycle, and that was fine with me. I enrolled at Wayne State University and began the curriculum, taking the required courses in the humanities, philosophy, art, and English. At the same time, I was working at an emergency medical clinic. It was a private clinic in the city run by three doctors. Two of the doctors were brothers, and the third was a heart specialist. The clinic was situated near the factories and primarily served men who got hurt on the job. I was hired to be the receptionist. I really didn't know anything, but the bookkeeper taught me the ropes, and I picked it all up quickly.

PART 2

# Marriage

# The Man of My Dreams

I WILL ALWAYS HAVE MEMORIES of the first apartment we lived in. It was a small one-bedroom apartment on the first floor. My parents slept on a Murphy bed in the living room. My sister and I shared the bedroom, and we slept in a double bed with a folded blanket between us to mark our territory. At night, as I waited in the quiet for sleep to come, I could hear a myriad of noises from our apartment building, whether it was the incinerator door opening and closing or snoring from the neighbors. When I was about ten years old, we moved from the back of the building to the front. It felt like such a huge step up. Even though Edythe and I still shared a room and a bed, I was excited that my parents now had their own bedroom as well. We also had a front porch. This particularly thrilled me; I enjoyed just sitting on that porch and observing life on the street. It would entertain me for hours. Just watching people and life go by still fascinates me. I am a people-watcher, and I love to observe others when they least expect it.

In the summer of 1951, when my parents had been married twenty-five years, my dad, my mother, and I moved into our first real house. A house in the suburbs with a yard was something we had all dreamed of. My mother was a great gardener, and after all those years of being in an apartment, it was wonderful to have a little garden. Whether it was a flower, a vegetable plant, or a tree, she would take a little snip and transplant it. Within a year something marvelous would bloom. She could make anything grow. I would often help her plant seeds and pick fruit, and I noticed everything she did to make the garden so lush. I loved flowers and gardens and dreamed of one day having my own house and a beautiful yard.

The summers were unbearably hot. One of my tactics for handling the intense heat was to run around in my short shorts. This was not lost on my neighbor, Al Seifman. Al was in the construction business, and after World War II he mainly added rooms onto homes. He and his wife, Shirley, had been living next door with their expanding family for several years. He adored my dad, and they were regulars at our house. He would see me in and out of the house with different boys, and he remarked that sometimes I had three dates over one weekend. I didn't know it at the time, but Al's mission was to get this virgin—me—married and off the block! The shorts were the catalyst for his plan. He began by setting me up on a blind date with a friend of his who was also in the construction business.

The night Al's buddy called to ask me for a date was one I will always remember vividly and will carry in my head and heart for the rest of my life. A voice, the most deliciously sexy and masculine voice I had ever heard, said, "Hi, Glorya. My friend Al gave me your number. I'm Don Kaufman." My stomach fluttered!

My mother was instrumental in helping me get ready to go out on all my dates. That night I went through many potential outfits but settled on a simple blouse and skirt with a belt that set off my waistline. But shoes—now, they were the critical part of the ensemble, and that's where Mom came into play. She had measured my height against the molding on the front door and carved two niches. One niche was my height while wearing heels, and the other niche was my height while wearing flats. God forbid I should be taller than my date. I was five feet five inches and my mother four feet nine inches. She was afraid I would never find a man that was taller than me. When Don arrived at the door, Mom came into my room and excitedly told me I could definitely wear my heels! Once I had primped myself to perfection and felt prepared, I headed out of my room to meet my blind date.

What I wasn't prepared for was the man standing in front of me in the entrance to our house. At six feet tall, he seemed to fill the room. I never really had thought about the expression "larger than life" until I met Don. That was Don. He was just as handsome and masculine as his voice over the phone had promised. He spoke a little louder than necessary. I found out later that he had lost 15 percent of his hearing in each ear from the noise of the planes he flew during the war. He had piercing blue eyes and a dazzling smile. I felt that it was a smile meant for me and me alone. I thought Don looked just like my favorite movie actor, Burt Lancaster. Years later, I met Mr. Lancaster at a party and told him that I had married a man who looked just like him. Intrigued, he raised his eyebrows, and when I pointed across the room to Don, he said, "Well, I'll be damned. You sure did." And with a wink he added, "You have great taste."

Don took me to a film at the Cinerama the night of our first date. It was a documentary, narrated by Lowell Thomas, about a plane flying over cities of the United States. In my estimation, Lowell's voice, deep and controlled, still paled in comparison to Don's. Before Lowell's voice had a chance to narrate what city the plane was flying over, Don already knew from the terrain and would whisper to me, leaning close and making my stomach flutter. I was so impressed! Our evening continued at Menjo's Restaurant where Don ordered us a lovely dinner. Interestingly, because Don was twelve years older, I was not asked for ID. In fact, I was I never asked for it again as long as I was with him. That night at Menjo's, Don ordered us champagne. Later he held me close on the dance floor, and I realized that he wasn't like any of the boys I had dated. In fact, he wasn't a boy at all. He was a man, a sophisticated, worldly adventurer! Every time I looked up at him, his beautiful blue eyes searched mine. There wasn't anything about him that didn't please my senses. I even loved the way he smelled.

Don was a gentleman in every way, and he left me at the door with a simple kiss on the cheek. I watched him drive away, and when my feet finally moved enough to take me inside, my dad, as usual, was waiting up to hear about my date. Dad and I were very close, and of course he was protective of his naïve daughter. I couldn't wait to talk with my dad when I got home. I was so taken with Don. "Dad," I said, "if I can get this guy, this is who I would like to marry."[2]

Don was as exciting and worldly as he was handsome. I knew Don was older than I was, but it wasn't until we were married and I saw his birthdate on our marriage license that I realized he was twelve years older. I'm not sure I would have dated him had I known he was that much older. I know for a fact that my parents would not have allowed me to date a man who was that much older. So thank goodness none of us knew! I also did not know he had been married twice before.

Don's early marriages took a toll on him. He was distrustful of women after his bad experiences. Sadly, this carried over to family dynamics and impacted generations to come in how he structured our home life and his estate plans. He made two major mistakes, in my book: setting up his will so that Eli Broad was executor, and stipulating that children born out of wedlock would not be entitled to an inheritance, which impacted our granddaughter April.

I knew from our first date that Don was the man for me. Given his experience with his two previous wives, he was gun-shy, but we were in love, and Don greatly enjoyed my family. He had always wanted children, and he knew that I was something special. After awhile, at Don's initiation, our conversations would turn to the shape and cut of diamonds. His sister Marian wore an emerald-cut diamond ring, and I was reluctant to speak up and tell him that I preferred a pear-shaped diamond. But eventually I managed, without insulting emerald-cut diamonds, to let him know my preference. A surprise was in store one magical evening when Don picked me up. My parents were home and hovered expectantly. Don proposed to me right there in the living room, handing me a ring. Don and my father were close and enjoyed each other's

---

2 My dad had talked me out of marriage proposals on more than one occasion. I had been dating a fellow who was accepted to medical school in Philadelphia. He proposed to me, and Dad's response was, "You really want to marry him and then work to put him through med school?" Many years later, after Don's death, my old friend contacted me and came out to California with his wife to attend the UCLA Gala for the opening of Kaufman Hall. We all went out to dinner, and to my astonishment he pulled out pictures of me as a teenager. He never knew that my dad had talked me out of marrying him.

company, so I was sure Dad knew that Don was going to propose. It did not surprise me that Don had discussed with my parents his plan to marry me. What did surprise me was the ring. It was the most beautiful ring I had ever seen, with a beautiful pear-shaped diamond.

I was so overwhelmed that it was hard for me to grasp at first that Don was proposing because he never actually asked the traditional question, "Will you marry me?" We were going to a special gala that night, and my first thought when I saw the ring was that perhaps it was for me to wear just for this special occasion. But that wasn't the case. I had turned down many marriage proposals, but they were all mere boys compared to this older and experienced man now asking me to be his wife. I was now sure that I had never been in love before Don Kaufman walked into my life. It was all happening to me, and I couldn't believe it. After all the pain and awkwardness I had endured growing up, Glorya Pinkis, a little cross-eyed girl from Detroit, was going to marry a handsome, exciting, and adventurous man. I was in love, and I felt like the luckiest girl in the world.

# Donald Bruce Kaufman

DONALD BRUCE KAUFMAN WAS BORN in Detroit to Russian immigrant parents, Sam and Celia Rose, who both suffered from health issues. Don's father, who grew up during the Russian pogroms, was malnourished and developed rickets. Perhaps as a result of calcium deficiencies, he was a very short man with a large head. The family was poor, and his father, a finish carpenter who did not like being away from his family, was often forced to take work out of town.

Don's mother suffered from schizophrenia, a mental disorder characterized by abnormal social behavior and an inability to understand reality. She also developed tuberculosis. Because of her illness, the government routinely sent social workers over to their house, and it was very important that everything be neat and clean for their inspection. Later, when Don became a cadet in the air force, all the boys were subjected to white-glove inspection. Cleanliness became a hallmark for Don, and when we were married, the cleanliness and neatness factor remained very important. He all but gave me the white-glove inspection.

Don, his brother, and his two sisters were sent to stay at the homes of different family members because his mother's health issues resulted in her frequent hospitalization. Don sold newspapers to help support the family. Even though his father was a strict Russian disciplinarian, Don, who was naturally adventurous, was left to his own devices, and he became a bit of a renegade and a daredevil to boot. He developed street smarts, driven by a desire to earn enough money to pay hospital bills. He missed out on a carefree childhood, and he would make up for this in his later years. Don loved his mother very much, and when she died at the young age of fifty-four, he was heartbroken and overcome with sadness and loss. He felt strongly that with more money he could have taken her to specialists who could have cured her. I thought it was very interesting, and a little sad as well, that throughout our marriage, he only mentioned his mother to me twice, telling me she was beautiful and kind. Even though it was not his fault, he still felt guilty about his inability to help. One of his deepest regrets was that she did not live to see his success.

Don was determined to make enough money to always be able to afford the best doctors and never again allow his loved ones to go without the best care available. Whenever one of our children suffered from even the simplest childhood malady, he would become concerned about whether we had the best doctors. He would hover until a fever broke or measles or chicken pox disappeared. It was sad and ironic that when our own daughter, Laura, developed schizophrenia, no amount of money or quality of care could cure her illness.

Don joined the marines right after high school. In 1943, toward the end of World War II, the air force opened its ranks to more volunteers, and Don quickly joined to become an aviation cadet. The boys all went through extensive training. When it came time for assignments, all the cadets were lined up wearing nothing but their dog tags. Too big and broad to be a pilot, Don was assigned to be a gunner, and the guy behind him—much smaller than Don—was assigned to be a pilot. The two exchanged dog tags discreetly, no one questioned Don's size, and he went on to serve as a pilot in the United States Army Air Corps.

As a teenager, Don worked as a laborer for a builder and learned how to frame houses, which got him interested in the building business. After the war, soldiers, sailors, and marines were all coming back home, ready to settle down, marry the sweethearts they left behind, and have families. Don started his own construction business to meet the demand: ABCO Construction. He created this name because it would appear first in the telephone-book listings. He worked as a general contractor, specializing in remodeling residential and commercial structures. While he gained invaluable experience on the job, Don also continued his education, studying engineering.

Because families were expanding rapidly, Don specialized in building home additions of all kinds: additional bedrooms, bathrooms, and recreation rooms. He was brilliant and innovative, continually developing new solutions to old problems. While he worked at additions and remodels, he was acutely aware of the need for affordable housing. What Don really longed to do was build homes from start to finish. And his goal was simple: to create and build homes that the average working man could afford.

When I met Don in 1952, he was buying lots in and around Detroit and working with an architect to build custom homes. He enjoyed great success in selling them as well. He was a hard worker, and putting in an eighteen-hour day was not unusual for him. He would immediately reinvest his money in the next building project whenever he sold a home, which did not leave him much liquidity.

A week before we were married, Don and I attended the wedding of my first cousin, Edye Lawson, and Eli Broad. We met them for dinner while we were both honeymooning in Miami Beach, Florida. We would see them at family functions, and the boys got to know each other. Eli, who had graduated from Michigan State University a few years earlier, was working as a CPA. He told Don that he was not happy with his job and wanted to go into business on his own. Don offered him space in our new office building on 8 Mile Road in Detroit. Eli was just starting out and did not have many clients in those early days, and Don was very busy. Eli saw an opportunity and asked Don if he could do his paperwork, thus saving Don a lot of time with waivers and with permits at the Building Department. The boys worked out an arrangement whereby Eli would provide services to Don in exchange for his office.

Eli asked Don if he would like to enter into a joint venture building low-cost houses. They shook hands to seal an agreement that they would each put in $25,000 to buy lots on the outskirts of Detroit. Since neither of them had that amount of money, they had to find a way to come up with their portions. Eli borrowed $25,000 from his father-in-law, my Uncle Morrie Lawson, and Don and I scrambled to come up with our half. I sold my 1954 aqua-and-white four-door Ford and a few pieces of my jewelry, and I closed a small bank account. Don added his small savings, and we were ready to go.

Don named their project "Award-Winning Homes by Kaufman and Broad" and worked with an architect to design two affordable models, while Eli handled the paperwork. Don spent endless hours at the jobsite, ensuring that every contractor did his job as expected. When the two model homes were completed, they were staged and opened to the public. The opening weekend, Eli, Edye, Don, and I went away together to Toledo, Ohio, where we spent the entire weekend biting our fingernails. It was an insufferably long weekend until a phone call brought us the news. To our delight and amazement, fourteen houses were sold based on the two models. People were literally lining up to purchase a Kaufman and Broad home. Kaufman and Broad was on its way to becoming a leader in the home-building industry.

I always had known that Don was a talented genius, but in my wildest dreams I had never before realized the extent of his ingenuity. In fact, Kaufman and Broad became the largest home-building company in the United States. It would soon become an international company, building in France. The company became famous for its low-cost homes in and around Paris, and the home office is now in La Defense.

The business that started with a handshake proved to be a very good partnership. While Eli met with bankers and scouted land for future building sites, Don was free to dedicate 100 percent of his time to creating and overseeing all construction phases. Don was an established builder when he brought Eli, a CPA with no building experience or background, into the business. Don's construction expertise and production know-how were the lifeblood of Kaufman and Broad. His skill at producing homes quickly and efficiently was the major contributor to the company's early success.

Always innovative in his field, looking for ways to attract more buyers and help them feel a part of the construction of their home, Don was the first to provide a one-year warranty on everything in the house, covering paint, plumbing, and anything else that might require repair. He was the first in Detroit to install appliances like refrigerators, stoves, washers, and dryers into new homes. He was the first to offer carpeting and three different color schemes. Attentive to the smallest detail, Don designed a kitchen island to the correct proportions for women moving about quickly so they would not be hurt by pointed counters. All of this was included in the price of Kaufman and Broad homes that were selling for between $13,000 and $15,000. Don was also the first to come up with the innovative idea of building homes on a slab and eliminating the basement, which cut the cost of each home significantly. A good idea travels quickly, and many builders followed Don's lead. He was well known as the "ideas" man, the creative force behind Kaufman and Broad's prowess in designing and building homes.

Don hired his father, Sam, to inspect all the homes, because he knew he could trust him. Sam was also in charge of customer satisfaction, and he took his job seriously. Even though he had been a very strict disciplinarian when Don was growing up, he learned during these years to appreciate the son who was to take very good care of him for the rest of his life.

Don was a master at coming up with home designs to match the money available. For years before he took Eli in, he dealt with the banks himself. While we were dating, we went to dinner with one of Don's bankers, who shared with us that he had experienced trouble with builders because they did not know what they were doing. Because Don stood behind his work, which was always superior, the banker wished that more builders were like him.

Even though Don had dealt with the banks in the early years, Eli took over this job, along with finding building sites. Like many business partners, they had their differences, and according to those who knew them, their relationship was stormy at times.

It is baffling to me that Don made Eli executor of his estate. This caused many problems for me and my children. In the sixties and seventies, it was common for men to exclude their wives from the family financial affairs, preferably entrusting their business management to other men. I was never privy to our financial status. If only he had made other choices and kept me informed, the subsequent battles over estate matters might not have occurred.

Given the way their partnership began, with such hope and creativity, it has been both sad and mystifying that Don's name was not carried forward by the company after his untimely death. Eli's public-relations firm and Eli himself have often failed to mention Don's name or to list Don as the cofounder of Kaufman and Broad. For me, it is morally wrong to fail to credit his mentor, particularly when the name of the company begins with "Kaufman."

"Kaufman" came first for a reason: Don was the company's visionary and its creative and driving force. To fail to mention Don and his role as cofounder is not OK with me. In 2006, *Forbes* magazine published an article stating that Eli Broad was the founder of Kaufman and Broad. I sent a two-page letter to Steven Forbes, CEO of *Forbes.* The letter outlined Don's work in the building business, culminating with the fact that Eli learned the construction business from his experienced partner, Don Kaufman, who should be listed as cofounder whenever the founding of Kaufman and Broad is mentioned. The reply I received to my letter was five lines long and stated that I was correct and that the "unfortunate oversight" would be rectified in their section entitled "Readers Say." My comments appeared in a small paragraph entitled "A Broader Story." I also had to contact Wikipedia to inquire as to why only Eli Broad was listed as founder of Kaufman and Broad. Don's name was not listed there either! At my insistence, Wikipedia staff put Don's name where it should rightfully be, as cofounder of Kaufman and Broad. I've learned to fight for the recognition that my late husband deserves, and I will never let his legacy go unacknowledged again. These experiences have also taught me a "broader" lesson, and that's to fight for whatever I believe in and deem worthy of battle.

Lou Berkowitz, Don's sister Marian's husband, credits Don with bringing him into Kaufman and Broad. Lou drove a truck as a furniture-delivery man. He was having a hard go of it when Don offered him a job. Don's idea was to have Lou put furniture in a model home to help potential buyers envision the living space.

Kaufman and Broad stock was handled by Bache & Co., which orchestrated a public offering over the counter before moving to the American Stock Exchange and later the New York Stock Exchange. Kaufman and

Broad was the first company to be traded on the New York Stock Exchange as a home builder (under the symbol KB) and was identified as one of the prestigious Fortune 500, the top five hundred money-making companies in America, from 2000 to 2008. Since its founding, the company had built 550 thousand homes primarily, as Don originally intended, for first-time home buyers.

At forty years old, Don made the decision to retire, though he still sat on the board of directors at Kaufman and Broad. He felt that he had made enough money and wanted to enjoy life and family. He valued the importance of money and loved to make it and be successful, but he clearly marched to the beat of his own drum and had his own notions of what constituted "enough money." For Don, "enough" meant having the money to take care of any family member who became ill; that was the driving force from his childhood.

In addition to knowing what it meant to have enough money, Don knew what it meant to enjoy life. It was easy for Don to sum up life: "Life is an adventure." The recipe for life in his eyes was a mixture of adventure, suspense, success, and family. One of his reasons for retiring at such an early age was that he had a list of "three hundred things" he wanted to do, and he wanted to be sure he had the time to get them done. He wanted to live life to the fullest, and his list of "things" included skiing, scuba diving, dirt-bike riding, mountain climbing, river rafting, and whatever else happened to whet his appetite.

In 1953 he read in the paper that Jacques Cousteau had invented the Aqua-Lung. He wrote to Jacques, told him he had a sports shop, and bought two Aqua-Lungs. Don flew to Miami with his friend Ben Takier, and they joined a group of deep-sea divers called the Pinder Boys and learned how to breathe with an Aqua-Lung. Don made several trips and learned how to dive, but he was never certified. Exciting and slightly harrowing trips were part of the adventure for Don, whether he was exploring Spanish galleons sunk in the Caribbean or taking a two-week trip down the Cataract Gorge of the Colorado River through the Grand Canyon in an open boat. For Don adventure was really a part of life—a thrilling part of life. He loved helicopter skiing in Canada, and he and our son Curtis jumped the cornice at Mammoth Mountains many times.

In 1967 Don met a fellow by the name of Herman Jensen, an explorer who traded in artifacts and was a member of the Adventurer's Club. Don always had a keen interest in archeology and primitive people, having previously explored Incan grave sites and ruins on the west side of the Peruvian Andes. It didn't take long for him to convince Herman to take him down the River. Exploring the back tributaries during a month-long safari, Herman taught Don to hunt small animals and birds with blowguns, and all the while Don was accumulating pre-Columbian artifacts for his archeological collection. Don kept track of the day's activities in his journal, taking voluminous notes. He said there were so many fireflies that he didn't know if he was up or down, and it gave him vertigo when he tried to sleep in a hammock on the riverbank. They followed their guides as they cleared a path through dense foliage and arrived each evening in small native villages. Don thought it was hysterical that Herman had a different wife in quite a few of these villages. He wanted Don to marry one of the women so she could wash his laundry. Don declined, saying he didn't mind doing his own laundry. He would later have our children mesmerized with his stories about the natives. They were small people, but their toes were like fingers and would curl and grab at things quickly. The natives swiftly guided Don and Herman through the jungle, their machetes expertly cutting through miles of gorgeous wild plants. Exhausted from trying to keep up with them in the humidity, Don reminded the guides that he and Herman were archeologists. The natives proceeded to stop occasionally, picking up heavy stones to show Don and Herman, which slowed the pace down a bit.

I had given Don some of my costume jewelry, some licorice, and a few other odds and ends to trade with the natives. He traded all these goodies for a baby ocelot. The sixties were not a time of high airline security, and Don managed to bring that little cat home in a duffel bag that he hid under his seat. Of course, the kids were excited at first, but the ocelot was not friendly; they were unable to become attached to him. He was a guest in our home for awhile.

The instinct of many cats in the wild is to excrete over water so that the scent is not detected by predators. I bought a portable child's toilet and put a little water in the removal pail at the bottom, hoping the cat would respond and use it. He did, propping himself up and sitting on the seat. It was an amazing sight. One day I opened the door and he made a dash for the outside, heading straight up a tall avocado tree! I was home alone with Stacie. I was unable to get him down and didn't know what to do. I asked a brave neighbor to help me. He fetched a tall ladder and heavy gloves and managed to get the cat down. This was all too much for me, and when Don returned home from a backpacking trip with the older children, I told him the cat had to go. We found a family who agreed to take him and honor our condition that our family could have visiting privileges. About a month later we all piled in the car and went to see the ocelot. When we arrived, we were shocked at the condition of the house. Furniture was shredded, sofas were torn up, and stuffing was everywhere. The cat, now a bit larger, sat on the buffet hissing at us. We didn't stay long. Needless to say, it was our first and last visit.

Don loved spending time with his children. His childhood had been difficult and creating a nurturing family culture was extremely important to him. He wanted to see his children grow up, not just look in on them as they slept, at the end of his workday. Much to their delight, he often went on adventures with each of them alone. One of his most harrowing adventures was a rafting trip down a rugged Canadian river with our son Curtis. The rapids were class four, and when they hit a huge hole, Don flew out the back of the raft. Curtis had just enough time to grab his arm before they hit another rapid. He held onto his father through several more harrowing rapids until finally they were able to pull him back into the raft. Curtis saved his father's life that day. As the boys would tell the story, Don was laughing the entire time. That was Don. Even when he was staring death in the face, he saw the humor in it. I know Don would subscribe to Hunter S. Thompson's view of life and death from *The Proud Highway: Saga of a Desperate Southern Gentleman, 1955–1967*:

> Life should not be a journey to the grave with the intention of arriving safely in a pretty and well preserved body, but rather to skid in broadside in a cloud of smoke, thoroughly used up, totally worn out, and loudly proclaiming...Wow! What a ride!

That was how Don lived, and it was indeed how he died. I have no doubt that for Don, death was but the next great adventure.

**Donald Bruce Kaufman and Eli Broad, late 1950s**

**Don as a young cadet**

# Wedding Bells and a New Life

In 1954, a year and a half after we met, Don and I were married. My mother and I designed my wedding dress, and then my mother made the dress and spent hours sewing on tiny pearls. It was really quite beautiful. More than thirty years later, it would be worn by my daughter-in-law Jill for her wedding to my son Curtis. I have since given the dress to USC and feel so honored that it will be on display as part of the Glorya Kaufman archives. Don and I had a beautiful formal wedding at the Lee Plaza Hotel in Detroit. Many of the 250 guests came in from Toronto for the occasion. Our wedding date, December 26, was selected by Don because in the building business all the contractors take off work for the holidays. He was always very committed to his work, so I was thrilled when he whisked me off to Florida for a ten-day honeymoon at the Fontainebleau Hotel.

What fun Don and I had. Each night was a romantic dinner complete with dancing under the Miami moonlight that I felt existed just for just the two of us. When the sun was out, it was one adventure after another. One of the most memorable occurred when Don rented a boat outfitted with both scuba and snorkel gear. While he enjoyed scuba diving, I stayed a great deal closer to the surface, snorkeling. As I snorkeled around near the boat having a lovely time looking at the colorful reef fish, I looked down to see a school of barracuda. When they breathe, their mouths open and close like a trap door, revealing their huge teeth. That was enough for me! Hyperventilating, I splashed my way back to the boat. I climbed aboard, and that's where I stayed for the rest of the day. I discovered later on, after telling my tale, that when they see and hear splashing, barracuda often attack.

Our honeymoon lasted ten unbelievably fabulous days and would be the first adventure of our twenty-eight years of trips for holidays, wedding anniversaries, and New Year's Eve celebrations.

After we were married I moved into Don's apartment at 2635 Cortland Avenue in Detroit, Michigan. At the end of World War II, the influx of so many returning servicemen made housing difficult to find. Don had rented a small apartment, but he had to buy the furniture that came with it. With one bedroom, a living room, a small kitchen, and old furniture, it was exactly the kind of home you would expect a bachelor who worked eighteen hours a day to have. I had my work cut out for me. I took a deep breath and rolled up my sleeves. I had fun fixing up the apartment; I went to Sears and bought nice covers for the sofa and chairs. I had a washing machine that fit into the sink in the kitchen, and that's how I washed clothes. It was hot and humid during the summer and hard to sleep at night. Don remedied this by putting books under the legs of the bed to lift it up in order to get the faint breeze from the open window, and we got a standing fan for the living room to circulate the air. Across the alley from our apartment was a Chinese restaurant, Atlantic Gardens. Our dining room and bedroom both faced the alley, and during the summer, between the humidity and still air, the smell of the Chinese food was always heavy, drifting into our bedroom. Unfortunately, Don had no remedy for that.

When Don and I married, I weighed ninety-five pounds and was really quite thin. My doctor advised me to wait a year and put on some weight before getting pregnant, but we wanted children right away. I conceived on our honeymoon. I wasn't strong enough to carry the baby full term, and labor had to be induced. Our first child, Laura Celia Kaufman, named after Don's mother, Celia Rose, was born premature on August 3, 1955. Due to her prematurity, she was born without eyebrows or fingernails, and her eye muscles quivered. But by the time she was four months old, she had developed into a blue-eyed beauty with light brown hair. I was busy with motherhood, and Don was putting in eighteen-hour work days, but we still managed to move to a little 1,500-square-foot house on Rosewood in Oak Park. We had a nice yard with a swing set, and, thank goodness, three bedrooms. Gayl Sarah was born November 9, 1956. Not long after Gayl was born I became pregnant with my third child.

Since we had sold my two-tone, four-door Ford for investment money, I had been without transportation for awhile, and I sorely needed a car. Don bought me a used 1948 Studebaker for fifty dollars. I was as thrilled as a teenager to have wheels, except my sweet ride had a major problem. Every time I drove over a bump in the road, the car would shimmy, and it would not stop shimmying until I pulled over and turned off the ignition and started the engine again. I would drive until I hit the next bump and repeated the same procedure. I mentioned the car's behavior to Don, but he did not seem overly concerned until the day his car was in the shop and I had to drive him to work. He was appalled when my car "did its thing," but, even more than that, I think he was actually embarrassed that he had not paid better attention to my complaint. He told me that the car was not safe, and we would have to have it repaired. He told me not to worry about the cost, but I always worried about the cost. I was cautious because my husband was frugal. There was a time I only served corn for dinner. When he asked me why, I told him I didn't have money to buy anything more. I had been dipping into my own bank account, and it eventually ran out of money. He asked why I didn't ask for money, and my reply was that I couldn't ask!

I was concerned that the repair would be expensive. I took the car to the mechanic, and after explaining the odd behavior, I waited while he set out to figure out the problem. It wasn't long before he came out and told me that the problem was fixed and I would not be encountering the problem again. I was relieved, but I held my breath while waiting for him to announce the cost of the repair. I was hoping it would not be more than the fifty-dollar purchase price of the car. The charge was twenty-five cents! A bolt was loose, and he tightened it! I decided that even though I didn't like to hear people complain, the next time I felt something needed attention I would be sure that Don heard me. It would be many more years before I became proficient at this endeavor.

**Left to right: Curtis, Gayl, Stacie, and Laura Kaufman**

# Edye Lawson Broad

I WAS ALWAYS VERY CLOSE to my dear cousin, Edye Lawson. She was named after the same aunt my sister Edythe was named after. We never met our aunt, as she died from cancer at the age of eighteen. I was four years older than Edye. When we were young, that made a difference in the relationship. My Uncle Morrie would often tell us that one day those four years wouldn't matter and we would become great friends. Uncle Morrie was right. We did indeed become great friends.

In addition to being smart, my Uncle Morrie was a chemist. He manufactured concentrated fruit syrups to put in soda drinks. On a visit to Uncle Morrie's factory I was mesmerized by the process and the aromas. He was a great role model for me as far as business is concerned. I always loved finding little jobs and earning my own money. It made me happy to be able to buy things for myself, whether it be fabric, patterns, a bike, or a car. Whenever I found a new job, I would call my Uncle Morrie and he would write a letter of recommendation, explaining what a hard worker I was and what a great asset I would be to any employer. With this help from Uncle Morrie, I would continually get little increases in salary. My dad was also in my corner when it came to improving myself or bettering my job. They both wanted me to increase my skills and expose myself to new environments, and my experiences at work did indeed develop my ability to get along with a wide range of coworkers, bosses, and customers.

I loved my Uncle Morrie and my cousin Edye. In those days there wasn't anything I would not have done for them. Edye told me that one of her biggest disappointments was that she couldn't attend my wedding because she was on her honeymoon. Edye and Eli were married the week before Don and I were. Actually, we had chosen the same date but changed it because Edye and Eli had chosen that date before us. Edye came to visit me in the hospital when I gave birth to Laura, and she told me the great news that she was pregnant. When I visited her in the hospital during the birth of their first boy, Jeff, I brought her the news that I was pregnant again. Unfortunately, this wonderful pattern of births and pregnancy declarations stopped there. Edye developed cancer and had a hysterectomy. She was the sixth person in the world involved in an experimental drug treatment, and her body went through horrific trauma. She would become ulcerated inside and out, and after a few months of rest, she would undergo the treatment again. I know how much she suffered physically and emotionally, and I so admired her bravery. Whenever I would visit or call her, she was always optimistic. I would say, "How are you today, dear cousin?" And she would reply with great cheer, "I have an M on my forehead today for Marvelous!" What a great attitude for a young girl in her twenties who was battling cancer and already knew that she couldn't have more children, or at least couldn't get pregnant and carry a child to term.

Edye desperately wanted another child, and Don and I set out to help them realize their dream. It touched me so much when Edye told me one memorable day how much she loved and admired me. Well, I felt the same way about Edye and was thrilled when I got the opportunity to show her the place she had in my heart. I already had my hands full with the girls, and just when I thought I had no more room on my plate, I decided I could make room to do something life-changing for Edye and Eli.

While I was still pregnant with Curtis and taking care of my two toddlers, Laura and Gayl, an attorney friend of ours located an unmarried, pregnant girl from Saginaw, Michigan, who did not wish to keep the baby. She was a lovely young college student who met a football player during her freshman year. Her due date was within a few weeks of my due date, and Edye and Eli's plan was to adopt the baby. Don and I agreed to take care of the young student during the pregnancy and have her live with us. We gave her our bedroom, our two girls shared a room, and our "new" master bedroom, or as I remember it, a glorified closet, was so small that in order to make the bed, I had to lie across it. She was a strong but sweet girl and would help me with Laura and Gayl. We were a family for seven months, but she was never told who was going to adopt the baby. I didn't see my cousin during this time. I kept our guest happy, well fed, took her to doctor appointments, and supported her original decision. She was no more than a child herself. Her baby was born ten days after Curtis. It was a difficult time for all of us. It was March and not the middle of summer, so at least we didn't have to deal with the heat and humidity.

After she gave birth, she told me she sang through the entire delivery and said she had no pain. One of the most difficult moments I have ever had to endure emotionally was holding this beautiful baby boy in my arms while his mother was sitting in a wheelchair in the elevator with me. When the elevator doors opened, we went our separate ways. I had helped do something wonderful for my dear cousin and her husband, which was emotional enough. But it was torturous for me to watch after the girl as she was wheeled out of the hospital and taken back to my house where her parents would pick her up and take her home. She never held or even set eyes on the beautiful baby she had just given birth to. Having just given birth myself, I could not imagine how devastated she must have been. While the young girl went home with her parents, her baby boy was taken to a foster home and immediately picked up by his new parents, Edye and Eli. The Broads were ecstatic to have their completed family together, and our two sons had been born just ten days apart. Gary Broad was a large and beautiful baby, and from the day he arrived home with his parents, he slept through the night. He grew up to be a beautiful young man, and I know he has been afforded all the luxuries and opportunities that come with being a Broad. As our children grew up together, our families shared many great trips and adventures. In addition to Edye and I being cousins and great friends, our husbands were business partners. Our time together was a mix of business, pleasure, and many relocations.

# Moving West, and West Again

IN 1960, I WAS PREGNANT with our fourth child. Don and I planned to name her after Don's favorite cousin, Lee Siegel, who had recently passed away. With such a growing family, we leased a larger house on Pine Lake in the Detroit area. We lived on a hilltop above the lake, and Don built a large cyclone-fence cage so the children could play safely, away from the lake's edge. While we were living there, we bought a thirteen-acre property on Pine Lake from a religious group and had plans to divide it into acre parcels and have family and friends buy lots and build their dream homes. Our plan was for nieces, nephews, and the children of close friends to all grow up together. We had beautiful architectural plans for our own dream home, but after Stacie Lyn was born, Kaufman and Broad had become so successful that we had to sell the property and abandon Pine Lake for our next adventure: Phoenix, Arizona. Before we moved, Eli and Edye moved to Phoenix with their two boys. While Eli scouted the new area for home locations, Don kept things going in Detroit. They really were a great team, and their duties were quite different. With his CPA background, Eli worked with the bankers, borrowed money for future projects, watched over the financial progress of the company, and scouted land for future home developments. Don knew the building business start to finish. He understood the difficulties of blue-collar workers and knew that just like anyone else, they wanted lovely homes with good schools nearby for their children. He worked with the architects in designing the homes and was on the job site overseeing the workmen every day. He was a perfectionist and only accepted the finest workmanship. Don and Eli loved what they were doing, building a company together from scratch, and I had my hands full with four children, who were between the ages of five and newborn.

Meanwhile, Edye was doing some scouting of her own in Phoenix, checking out preschools, local doctors, and shopping opportunities. We all teased Don for many years to come after he offered Edye one hundred dollars a month to keep me out of beautiful clothing stores! Our two families were very close in those days, and we had a lot of fun together. In addition to giving him the opportunity of a lifetime and showing him the ropes of the building business, Don got Eli interested in skiing and tennis. Edye was not a sports enthusiast; her hobby was reading. While the three of us would be on the slopes or the tennis courts, Edye was happy to snuggle up with a great book. We had such fun entertaining her over dinner with our athletic tales of the day.

Before we joined the Broads in Phoenix, Don and I discussed having more children. I thought six was a good number—probably an offshoot of my childhood plans for an orphanage—but Don thought four was plenty. So that was it for more children. Luckily, he was older and wiser; in time, I knew he was right! While I stayed behind in Detroit with the four children, Don found our new home in Phoenix, just three blocks from Scottsdale. I saw our new home at 3732 East Pierson Street for the first time when we arrived in Phoenix. It was really quite lovely, and I knew that I didn't have to worry about not liking a home that Don selected. We lived in a hotel for several months while the upgrading and painting of the new home was completed. Edye had found Camelback Desert Nursery School for our older children to attend along with her boys. Our CPA, Leroy Goldman, and his wife, Anne, and their children also relocated to Phoenix with us. Between the three families and nine small children, we were quite an extended family and did not feel the sting of loneliness that most people might experience upon relocating to a new state with different weather and new surroundings. For all of us, it was a new beginning, and we were all ready to tackle the adventure.

I loved Phoenix. The sunsets were beautiful and we had fifteen grapefruit trees in our backyard. These simple things—sunsets and grapefruit trees—were such wonderful novelties for a family used to living in the cold and snow.

My children thrived in Arizona. The weather was always glorious, and my son Curtis was so active that we had to devise a plan so that he could expend some of his energy. We bought large rubber-tire tubes and placed them around the yard among the trees and challenged Curtis to run and jump over them. He had great fun, and our plan worked: He eventually tired!

Once we were all settled in and Don was back to working eighteen hours a day, I decided to embark on one of my own personal adventures: going back to finish college. I enrolled in Arizona State University–Tempe and took as many classes as I could in the little spare time I had between the four children and everything that comes with running a household. Even though I was married, I was still in my twenties and felt that I fit right in with the younger college students. I loved being back at school, and my goal was to absorb all the knowledge I could from the many interesting professors. I managed to have the young boys carry my books for me, and they even came over to study together at the kitchen table. Don got a kick out of the whole scene and was very encouraging about my studies.

While I attended classes, it comforted me to know that Esther, a woman we had brought with us from Detroit, was home to care for and watch the children. Esther Slivinski was a nice Polish girl with bad teeth and strabismus, the same eye disorder I suffered from as a child. Don and I took her to our dentist and had her teeth fixed, and we also had her eyes corrected. We treated her like family, and it was sad and very disappointing to us when she began to party and drink too much. We had to let her go, and with such young children it was hard to find a trustworthy replacement, but I managed. I had to. When Don and I would go away alone for a ski trip, my folks would come out to Arizona and stay with the children. Ann Goldman's mother was also a great sitter and would help us out on occasion. She was a wonderfully kind woman, and she loved to cook. The kids loved her, especially Curtis, who would call her "Mr. Goldman." We lived happily in Phoenix for three years, but we then moved to Huntington Harbour in Huntington Beach, California.

Kaufman and Broad was continuing to expand, this time to California. In addition to homes, the company was building condominiums and also held several government contracts. The Broad family moved to Brentwood, but Don wanted to be next to the ocean, so our choice was Huntington Harbour, right on the water. We lived on Edgewater Lane, located on one of the canals overlooking the clubhouse. One of Don's dreams was to have a little speedboat, and now that we lived on the water he was intent on getting a boat. Our salesman took us to the home of a gentleman who wore very thick glasses. He had the habit of taking his yacht out, drinking too much, and falling overboard. His wife insisted that he sell the forty-three-foot *Chris Craft*. This was not the little speedboat Don had envisioned, but we had gone along with the salesman just to make him happy. Don told the gentleman he was absolutely not interested, but when the salesman insisted on knowing what Don would pay for the yacht, Don threw out the low amount of $18,000. The gentleman jumped for joy, telling us we could have the yacht for that amount, even though he was asking $40,000! We were now the proud owners of a yacht that slept six—and I had even more on my overcrowded plate.

The *Chris Craft* was parked on the canal in front of our house. It was in a vulnerable spot, right where the racing boats would turn and bump into it. Between the repairs from accidents, barnacle removal, and the huge task of maintaining a yacht, it was as much work as having another child. At the time, the Huntington Harbour bridge was so low that we could only take the boat in and out at low tide. One time, Don took the children for a day on the yacht but couldn't get back under the bridge for many hours; they had to wait for the tide to recede. The tower called me and kept me informed, but I was a nervous wreck thinking of him out there with our four active kids. Somehow that yacht managed to stay with our family for several years. Eventually Don recognized that it was more work than fun, and he sold it.

The kids were getting older, and I had some time to attend classes at UC–Irvine. I really enjoyed my continuing education, and I also managed to fit in duties as a Cub Scout leader for Curtis and a Campfire leader for the girls. My friend Marilyn Tom was a coleader with me, and we had great fun organizing activities for the kids; in fact we have remained friends all these years. Between these activities, taking the kids for various art and music lessons, and Don's long hours, there was no time for social activities. Kaufman and Broad was growing by leaps and bounds, and Don would frequently share his ideas with me.

Our home was lovely, and we loved being near the water. But we had become disenchanted with the schools, which seemed to be dominated by the John Birch Society. The last straw was when one of Gayl's teachers told the class that if they lived in Sol Vista, they were lower class, and if they lived in Huntington Harbour, they were upper class. When Gayl came home and announced, "I didn't know we were upper class," that pretty much did it for me and Don. We finally found a great school in Fullerton, but I had to drive forty-five minutes each way to take the children to school. Three hours a day in the car was just too much, so Don and I spent that summer scouting for a home that would meet our many requirements. We wanted sidewalks so the kids could walk to school. We wanted a library nearby and a neighborhood with other Jewish children for our kids to grow up with. By the time we had found a home and neighborhood that fit the bill, it turned out to be in the heart of Beverly Hills.

At this point we had already moved Don's father and lady friend to a retirement community, Leisure World, in Seal Beach, quite close to Huntington Harbour. It was a wonderful place, and it was still only an hour or so from Beverly Hills. I really wanted to get my parents out of the cold weather of Detroit and move them to the warm and sunny retirement climate of Southern California—and, of course, closer to me and the family. Don and I bought my folks a condo at Leisure World in Laguna Beach, just south of Seal Beach, and they were happy there. Don told my father he would be picking up the tab. When my father argued with him, Don basically told him it was his treat, and he was to accept that and enjoy his retirement. They lived there for about fifteen years, and I was so happy to be able make them happy and comfortable.

Dad really loved living at Leisure World and would play cards, especially gin rummy, with his cronies. He always brought along donuts and his winning smile. My dad's sweet tooth was his downfall, but it was also a constant source of amusement. My mom loved to bake fresh pastries to have around in case of visitors, and her specialty was rugelach. One morning I drove down to visit, and as Mom and I talked in the kitchen, Dad watched the news in the living room. I was getting a kick out of Mom's storytelling. She said that she had baked a large batch of rugelach and put them in a tin to keep in the freezer. If she had not frozen them, my dad would have eaten them all. After many weeks, she remembered the frozen rugelach. To her surprise when she opened the tin there were only two pieces of pastry left. She ate them and put the tin back in the freezer with a note inside. The note said, "Ha, Ha." She said Dad never mentioned the note or that the last two rugelach were gone. I called Dad into the kitchen and confronted him. All he could say was "What rugelach?" He finally broke down and admitted his thievery. But what struck me as funny was his shrug of the shoulders as he said, "Glorya, you know your mother just doesn't have a sense of humor." It was a gentle way my parents had of teasing each other, and I got a laugh out of it.

With or without rugelach, my parents were really thriving in Leisure World. My dad loved telling his pals stories about the good old days in Miami Beach. Every winter my parents would rent a condo and meet up with friends and relatives from Toronto to enjoy the sunshine and the great restaurants like Wolfie's, the famous delicatessen. They would come home tan and rested and full of wonderful stories. At Leisure World, Mom had a great little garden out back of the condo that she nurtured just as she did at our little house in Detroit—only now she had a warm climate to enjoy. She took up ceramics and painting, and she made some lovely friends. My parents would enjoy bus trips to various locations, live bands, and ballroom dancing on Saturday nights. They made an unforgettable trip to the taping of Johnny Carson's *Tonight Show*. It made Don and me so happy to know our folks were not only nearby but also enjoying their retirement years.

After Don's death, I asked my friend Harriette Craig to accompany me to Leisure World for an evening of music and dancing with the elders. She was game, so we dressed up, and off we went. The music, mostly from the fifties and sixties, was wonderful for dancing. Dad loved fast music with lots of rhythm, and he wasted no time getting me on the dance floor to show off for his cronies. Harriette was asked to dance, and we were having a ball. Over the course of the evening, Harriette and I never sat down as the elderly gentlemen lined up for their turn to dance. After one of the gentleman danced, he sat down, gasping for air. On the way home I said to Harriette, "I don't think we should go back again. If he didn't have a heart attack, then we performed a mitzvah. If he did have a heart attack, we might have killed somebody!"

**My parents, Eva and Sam Pinkis**

# A New Zip Code

By the time we moved into our Beverly Hills home on Rexford Drive, I had become an expert mover. I labeled all the boxes with room and/or child designation, and for the most part, all the moving in and organizing was up to me. Edye was kind enough to take the kids for the day while I worked on the house. Don had already retired from Kaufman and Broad, but he was about to go on hiatus from retirement—for a week. Eli had begged him to. Eli was desperate for a new model home to be on the market as soon as possible, and he needed Don to do what no one else could: build a brick house in a week in the freezing cold of Detroit! Don and his crew started on a Friday, using frost rippers to tear through the ground, and Don pushed every step of the way. One week later, a brick house was finished and furnished, with buyers walking through talking to salesmen. Over the years Don would say, "I still hear about that one in the business...a full-basement house in a week." He deserved to be proud, and he headed right back to retirement.

Life in our new home in Beverly Hills was moving full speed ahead. We bought the house from a kind gentleman named Sam Franklin, who was the father of the actress Bonnie Franklin. It needed some work to accommodate our needs, but the most fantastic feature was located on the third floor of the house: a most wonderful room with a wooden floor and a dance barre. The girls were all taking ballet classes, and I loved yoga, so the room became our special dance space. The yard had a beautiful pool, and Don had built a tree house for the kids next to two wonderful avocado trees. Our dog Troy, who had developed the most amazingly shiny coat, was also getting fatter. One day I realized he was eating the avocados as they dropped from the trees, ripe and delicious—and fattening!

The kids were offered lessons in most anything they chose, from ballet to piano to swimming. Curtis loved his drum lessons but wouldn't practice, so the lessons stopped. Don and I had a philosophy that the children be afforded any and all opportunities we could provide, but they had to do their part and apply themselves and practice. There was no negotiation, however, when it came to schoolwork. That had to get done without fail. I helped them a lot, testing them for exams and making flashcards for math and English. When Curtis had a project due on Japan, we went to a travel agency together for brochures, and I helped him put together his project. He was so pleased to get an A+. So was I! The kids were growing up fast, and all four of them were in school. I would watch from the front door as Curtis and Stacie walked to school together, holding hands. It was a lovely time in our lives, and the family was thriving. I decided it was time for me to get back to my own classes, and I enrolled at UCLA.

While Don loved his children and included them in just about everything we did, we still enjoyed many adventures together as man and wife. I was always ready for the next adventure, whether it be renting a motor bike in Hawaii and touring the island for nine hours or a ski trip for just the two of us. While we were living in Beverly Hills, Don and I enjoyed one of our most wonderful vacations as a couple. Our destination was at a Club Med on Moorea Island, just northwest of Tahiti. Not only was it a fabulous trip, but I would meet someone who would become a close friend.

**The Kaufman family and Troy**

**Stacie and Gayl practicing at the ballet barre**

# Tahiti

THERE IS ONLY ONE CIVILIZED thing to do when waiting for a shuttle boat: Find the nearest bar and order something wildly cold, fruity, and delicious. After arriving on the island of Papeete, Don and I did just that while we awaited our shuttle to the island of Moorea. Don and I had just been served two of the fruitiest drinks I had ever tasted, and I struck up a conversation with a delightful woman also waiting for the shuttle. Rita Kaplan was a child psychologist from New York traveling alone for the first time in her life. I thought this was very brave of her, and I liked her immediately. She was divorced, with four children whom she had just put through college. My four were still walking off to school hand in hand, and I admired the fact that all her children had a college education. I knew the work, devotion, and sacrifice it must have taken to accomplish this.

In between wonderful water sports and tropical evening dinners at the beautiful Club Med, Rita shared with me the sadness and grief that she felt. Her lover had died in her arms just a few weeks before the trip, and she told me that she had just had to get away.

Rita had a lovely home on Long Island, and even though geography kept us apart, we kept in touch. I would soon learn from Rita about Larry Spina, a very attractive hairdresser who owned his own salon. He was a delightful Italian man with not only a great sense of humor but also a gorgeous head of hair. How lucky could a girl get? They fell in love; however, Rita felt some trepidation. She was afraid that perhaps Larry would not fit in with her group of intellectual friends. Delightfully, she was wrong. All her friends adored Larry, and Rita plowed ahead with the relationship. They were soon married. Larry sold his business, and Rita sold her home. Throwing caution to the wind again, they did something neither had ever done. They bought a boat and called it *Trial Run*. Rita continued with her practice, and Larry cooked and took care of everything else.

During the summers they would venture out to sea, but when winter set in they were docked on the water in Huntington, New York. On one memorable occasion, I went to stay with them. I was very nervous because Don was picking up his new bi-wing airplane, *Witch Hawk*. It was a stunt plane, similar to those used in World War I, and Don was very excited. He was a passenger on the flight, which only seated two, and he learned to fly the plane that day. Rita and Larry were reassuring and comforting, and they kept me busy until we got the call that Don had arrived safely home in Los Angeles.

Larry and Rita came to California to visit us, and we planned a large catered dinner party at the ranch. We had just suffered a wildfire, which had destroyed immense quantities of vegetation, and the day of the party we were deluged with torrential rains that flooded our canyon. We had to cancel the party and instead sent the food to the Paul Revere School to feed the neighbors evacuated because of the threat of mudslides. Don and Larry were great friends, and both had a way of making the experience fun.

When Don was killed, I made two phone calls to friends. One was to Peggie Gill, a close friend and mentor, and the other was to Rita. Rita told me they could either come the next day or wait for a few weeks when the visits from other friends dwindled. They did just that, the latter, and they were with me on my birthday, January 23, which was comforting.

When I told Rita I would like to take them to a certain restaurant or place, she would say, "Was that a favorite place of yours and Don's?" I would say, "Yes." Then she'd say, "No, we are going to find new places and new experiences. I want you to change the habits that you and Don had together." Rita taught me to change my patterns and to replace all the familiar things that Don and I had shared for twenty-eight years. Still, there were many tears. The memories were so deeply embedded that truly in my heart I did not know if I could move on without Don. He was my breath, my life. I knew nothing else but to abide by his ways and take care of my family. I was in limbo. The coping skills and strategies for changing my patterns that Rita taught me were not only wise, they were invaluable to my recovery.

Many years later, Rita and Larry came to visit me on their way to San Francisco. They were headed to care for their grandson while Rita's daughter Nancy took continuing-education classes to maintain her psychology degree. They stayed with me at Amber Hills, and I had some friends over for dinner. It was a lovely evening, and we were all so happy to be together. My guests were excited for me because I was planning a cruise to Indonesia later in the year and, as I had done when visiting both St. Moritz and India, I planned to travel alone. They left the next morning for San Francisco. When I received a message a few days later to call Rita, I returned her call and received devastating news. Larry had been playing tennis with Nancy's husband when he suffered a heart attack and died immediately. I left as soon as I could to be with Rita in San Francisco. Before returning home, I gave Rita a note asking her to be my guest on the cruise. She was hesitant, but her children encouraged her and she came with me.

Our ship, the *Seaborne*, was small enough that we were able to get to know most of passengers. Each day was a different excursion to a different island. In addition to exploring Bali, we visited ancient temples and toured the palace of the King and Queen of Kerambitan. The Komodo dragons were a highlight on the island of Komodo. The largest living species of lizard, they can grow to ten feet in length, and they weigh in at 150 pounds. We had a wonderful time, and the trip was healing for both of us. We were there for each other.

Rita now suffers from dementia and is in a care facility. I will always remember her jet-black hair and marvelous blue eyes. To me, she always looked like the actress Jean Simmons. I carry her in my heart, and I will always think of her as the woman who was a special friend and a very special teacher. How I miss her.

**Stacie and Curt Kaufman sitting in *Witch Hawk*, Gayl and Glorya Kaufman beside the plane**

# The Ranch: Amber Hills

A FEW YEARS AFTER OUR fabulous Club Med vacation when we were all still living happily in Beverly Hills, Don came home one day and announced that we were going to be even happier. He had taken the children horseback riding at Crestwood Riding Stables in Brentwood. The trails went up on the ridge and at one point, riding along the crest of the mountain, they looked down at what appeared to be an oasis—a beautiful and secluded piece of property dotted with many shady trees, complete with a huge lake and a waterfall. They rode down the mountain and encountered the owner, Dr. Fred Worden. Don introduced himself and asked if his place was for sale. Dr. Worden said it was not. In fact, he said, "I will move from here when they carry me out in a casket." Such an answer was never a "no" to Don—just a challenge. The property also included a beautiful tennis court that had Don salivating. I knew one way or the other we were destined to be the new owners. With a little manipulation, Don and I found ourselves invited to a cocktail party that would change our lives. Dr. Worden and his wife, Kay, the heiress to the 3M Company, were strong Democrats, and we didn't realize until we arrived that it was a political affair. One of their guests was Tom Bradley, an African American politician who would soon be running for mayor on the promise of rebuilding the LA metro system. Among the guests were some VIPs from Harvard who were trying to seduce Dr. Worden into joining them back East. And there were Don and I, the couple whose objective was to buy the Wordens' home. Dr. Worden was not carried out in a casket; he simply took the Harvard offer, and in the summer of 1969, we became the proud owners of "The Ranch", 3100

Mandeville Canyon Road, a forty-eight-acre estate in the heart of Brentwood that would acquire its colorful name years later. My first thought was, *What have I gotten myself into?* It was a huge piece of property, and in order to buy the place, we had to purchase all of their large, heavy, Early American furniture, which was not my style. Making the place our home would take some elbow grease. But once again, I rolled up my sleeves and went to work without complaint.

Our lives were oriented toward animals and nature in general, and we loved it that way, so we put up with the environmental risks of fire and the Santa Ana winds. Just when I thought I couldn't work any harder and the children couldn't be any happier, we were presented with an opportunity we couldn't pass up. Jungleland, a zoo in Thousand Oaks, was out of funds and could no longer feed and care for the many animals on the property. In December of 1969, there was an auction to sell all of their animals and birds, and quite a few ended up at the Kaufman ranch. The children loved the two little miniature horses we rescued. A mischievous little black rascal we named Little Bit would grab tools from the gardener's pockets and take off with them, throwing them into the lake! The other miniature horse was a sweet and beautiful brown-and-white paint, even a bit smaller than Little Bit. She was like a little stuffed animal and loved to be cuddled. When we would watch her from a distance up on the hill, she looked full grown. Not long after she came to our home, Don found her dead at the lake's edge. She had been attacked and killed, and we assumed it was a coyote as our mountains were full of them. However, a later incident proved that it was our German shepherd, Troy, who had attacked our little mini. Troy was a trusted family member, and it was hard for all of us to imagine and then accept that he could have been the culprit. Don was on his way to get his rifle and kill Troy when Stacie intervened. She cried to her dad that it was Troy's instinct, and that it wasn't his fault. Don loved Troy, but he was afraid that now that he had killed once, Troy could do it again, or that he could take down a small child. But Troy's life was spared that day, thanks to Stacie, and he lived to an old age, never harming another animal.

We also selected several blue peacocks at Jungleland, but they weren't caged when we arrived to pick them up, and we could not catch them. They may still be in Thousand Oaks, living in the treetops among the residents. Our lake was a perfect home for the seventy white ducks, geese, and mallards we selected, but when the white ducks and geese shed their feathers, the lake appeared to be covered in snow! We talked it over and decided to donate the ducks and geese to Synanon, a rehabilitation center in Santa Monica that actually was later revealed to be a violent cult. Hopefully the ducks were not converts.

The animal that stands out the most was the three-month-old lion cub that we named Samson. When we first brought Samson home, Don and I told the children it would only be temporary, but they were so busy bottle-feeding him I'm sure it didn't sink in. If they did hear, I'm sure they figured we would have a change of heart. Well, that would only have happened if the little lion cub didn't have plans to grow into ferocious lion. An exotic animal vet kept an eye on him, educating us on how to handle a lion. We bought special food for our growing family member, and we bottle-fed him. We learned a great deal about the habits and instincts of wild cats. When they hunt down prey and want to attack, they approach from the back, never facing their prey. When Curtis and his friends would allow Samson to play football with them, he would chase the boys, sometimes taking a nip from their pants. We kept Samson for about eight months and after many tears on the part of the children, Samson went on to a new home at Holter's Ranch in San Bernardino. Holter's Ranch was a facility that trained wild animals for the film industry. We all piled in the mobile home and drove Samson to his new home. Years later, when I found a pair of torn jeans in Curtis's room, I went to throw them out until he stopped me, telling me that they were a souvenir of his beloved Samson.

It wasn't until forty years later, when I began to compile material for this book that I came across an old movie called *The Roaring Kaufmans*. When we first moved into the ranch in 1969, Don had hired a professional photographer to follow our family around the ranch. How nostalgic it was to see how much fun we all had. One of the highlights was the children playing and wrestling with Samson. I marveled at how Samson got along with our German shepherd, Troy, and our little terrier, Scampi. We took turns riding with Don on his motorcycle, once four of us at a time. For our kids the ranch was like an amusement park. We slid down the fireman's pole, flopped about the trampoline, and dumped one another from the hammock. It was pure fun. Don was very macho and dominant, picking up Samson by the tail and scruff of his neck and placing him on top of the car for the children to fuss over. It is so funny to see that through all of this, my hair was done in a French twist. It's not so funny to see was how peripheral I was in the movie. In the thirty minutes, I was only seen three times. That was the way of my life in those days. I was very much in the background.

It was time for me to do something for myself that would prove to be a lifelong love affair. I took up painting, something I had always wanted to do but had never had the time to pursue. I had been taking classes at UCLA, still working toward my Bachelor of Arts. The requirements were becoming very difficult to fulfill, as the classes I was taking at various campuses didn't always transfer. It was at a Fourth of July party that I attended with Don that I met a delightful French woman who told me all about the oil-painting classes she was taking. Gabby Rifkind convinced me to join her in her art class. The wonderful teacher, Dino Sider, taught me everything I know about oil painting. The class varied from between five and eight people, and I attended a two-hour class once a week. We could choose what we wished to paint, and Dino would guide us through our individual journeys. He was a great artist but a bit on the lazy side, and he definitely enjoyed cocktail hour more frequently than just at cocktail hour. I will always be grateful to him; he helped me fulfill something just for me. I like to think that I returned the favor. When I first took his class, he was no longer painting himself. I am not sure of the reasons, but I gleaned that it was because he had lost a love. He liked my imagination and my work, and he soon began painting again. I was quite thrilled for him, and all of us in the class were very happy to see a brush in his hand once more. I love to paint colorful spheres, and he began to paint spheres also, but only white on white—perfectly, outrageously wonderful! My painting inspired him, and I was thrilled.

I forced myself to continue to paint with Dino after Don's death, and then I found myself having to deal with Dino's death. Evidently he was home alone, had a heart attack, and died, and he wasn't found for several days. He had no family, so several of us from art class got together and had a service and burial. I was so sad that he was alone at the end of his life.

I attended the closing ceremony of the 1984 Olympics and was inspired by its forty-five minutes of breathtaking fireworks. I went home and painted fireworks in pastel oils to blend with my pastel bedroom colors, soft shades of lavender, pink, lime green, and blue. This painting still hangs in my bedroom and provides a burst of energy when I awaken every morning. I'm very proud of my work and get many offers for my paintings or commissions for new pieces. I have only wanted to paint for my own pleasure and enjoyment but am honored by the compliments. After Don's death and before Dino passed away, he painted a very demure portrait of me in a rose-colored dress. I look quite sad in the painting, which is understandable. I donated it to the USC Kaufman School of Dance, and I know Dino would be proud that his portrait of me has a place of honor—and he also occupies a place of honor in my heart. I tried other art classes after Dino's death, but it just wasn't the same. I still love the smell of oil paints and would love to get back to painting again one day.

Back when Dick Powell and June Allyson owned the Amber Hills property, and for many years after that, the ranch was used for episodic television filming. In the 1960s many popular shows used the ranch as a location. The ABC television series *Hart to Hart* began filming on the property in 1979. After Don's accident, I told Universal Studios that I no longer wanted them to film *Hart to Hart* at the ranch. I was uncomfortable because within a year and a half, three horrific tragedies had befallen people connected to the ranch and the series: Natalie Wood, R. J. Wagner's wife, drowned, Stephanie Powers's friend William Holden fell, hit his head, and died, and Don was killed in the plane crash. The filming was a painful reminder of happier days before the accident.

Many years later I decided to move to be closer to my projects with USC and the Music Center; the traffic along Sunset was becoming unbearable. My beautiful Amber Hills went up for sale with Eli Broad at the helm as special trustee. Eli chose to go with the broker who had already failed to sell the estate across the street from mine for several years, eventually selling it at auction for a very low price. The same situation occurred with my estate. Amber Hills was ultimately sold at auction as well for a shockingly small amount. The saddest part for me was what happened to our beloved ranch. Eli had given J. P. Morgan responsibility for the property maintenance. The company allowed Amber Hills to be run into the ground. It hired an inexperienced landscaper who had only recently acquired a license. This person decided to remove all 550 rosebushes and all the beautiful crepe myrtles and trumpet trees. It was heartbreaking for me. I look back with fondness on those years at Amber Hills, but my memories are bittersweet reminders that I cannot always be in control; inevitably, life changes.

## Deborah Schwartz: Lifelong Friend and Coauthor

For some time, I had boarded my horse at what would become the Kaufmans' Brentwood estate. One day in 1969 I went cantering down the mountainside next to the driveway to see a car slowly come to a stop next to me. Windows were rolled down, and four children, ranging from nine to fourteen years in age and with huge smiles on their faces, scrambled for a closer look at me and my horse. A beautiful red-haired woman wearing oversize sunglasses patiently waited, a beautiful, sweet smile on her face, as she enjoyed her children fawning over me and my horse. This was my introduction to the Kaufman family. It wasn't until a few days later that I was to meet probably the most colorful, most daring, most dashing, and unbelievably fun father figure ever: Don Kaufman, to me Mr. Kaufman.

Unbeknown to me at the time, Mrs. Kaufman would become my friend and would be a mother figure to me, even when I was well into my sixties! Mr. Kaufman would introduce me to his friends as "the kid who came with the barn." And, of course, the four Kaufman children became my "siblings," especially Gayl, the second oldest. We were best friends for many years to come.

Mrs. Kaufman was the ever patient mom, and I would marvel at how calm she could stay. Mr. Kaufman, a little hard of hearing, always talked about ten times louder than necessary. He would burst into the kitchen, talking up a storm while Mrs. Kaufman tried to hold a phone conversation. Instead of losing her cool, she simply placed a hand over her ear and continued talking. In that moment, she became my poster child for patience. I sat watching how calm and peaceful this beautiful woman could stay while her family noisily buzzed about her. I loved nothing more than going into her walk-in pantry and admiring all the food. I never saw so much food in one place except in a market. Mrs. Kaufman kept that pantry brimming for her family. I looked around the fun kitchen and the formal dining room and remembered the first meal I had at the Kaufmans' table.

It would be on these lazy, fun-filled, and carefree afternoons that Mrs. Kaufman would arrive home from doing many errands. We would know she was coming because we would hear her car come over the bridge, and the dogs would bark and run to greet her. There was just no getting out of your car at the ranch without three dogs trying to pile in at the same time! Now, when it came to shopping, Mrs. Kaufman was a professional. She didn't just shop for herself, but she shopped for the entire family.

The girls and I would run to greet her at the car, hoping she had been shopping at Loehmann's. Mrs. Kaufman always dressed stylishly, if not expensively, and she could afford to shop anywhere she liked, from Neiman Marcus to any trendy store on Rodeo Drive in Beverly Hills. But for her, a deliciously fun afternoon was a shopping trip to Loehmann's, a wonderful discount store in the San Fernando Valley. We would all crowd into the master bedroom to see what she had bought.

The thing I found totally wild about Mr. and Mrs. Kaufman's room was that their master bed had controls that allowed the head and foot of the bed to move independently on each side. I had never seen such a thing before. But the other innovative thing that blew my mind at the time was that they each had a separate television, with head phones, above each side of their bed in the ceiling! Because Mr. Kaufman was hard of hearing, he could have his volume as loud as he wanted, and they could watch different shows and fall asleep whenever they wanted. Between the ear phones and the eye mask that Mrs. Kaufman wore, I'm sure they were a sight to see. It's one I never laid eyes on, but for me, the Kaufmans were the most amazing ever.

Looking back, I truly don't know how Mrs. Kaufman juggled everything in her life with such grace. Between the demands of four children, Mr. Kaufman being retired and buzzing about at home every day, the responsibilities of the home, and the lovely but overwhelming vastness of the ranch property, I still marvel at how she never dropped the ball. Then you factor in kids like me hanging about and staying for meals and maybe for the night—or the weekend—and I figure she was just about ready for canonization.

## Margaret Pace: Lifelong Friend

Shortly after I married my husband, Russell, we were invited to a party at the old Robert Taylor estate across the street from the Kaufmans' ranch in Brentwood. Little did I know that I was about to make a friend for life: Glorya Kaufman. My first impression of Glorya was that she was warm and caring, with a great sense of humor. I felt comfortable with her immediately; it was as if we had been friends for years. Our friendship grew, and in addition to lunches and dinner parties, Glorya invited me to join a group of women for an art trip to Paris. Glorya had always wanted to paint but had always put husband and children first. She had been studying oil painting and taking classes several times a week with an instructor she loved, Dino Sider. Her work was fantastic, and I truly feel it was the first time in her life that she was following a dream of her own. It was a tremendously creative outlet for her and many of her best works hang in her home today. She donated the remainder of her artwork to the University of Southern California, where the pieces hang proudly in their offices.

I did not realize it at the time, but the art trip to Paris was the first time Glorya would be traveling outside the country, and—what's even more interesting—it would be the first trip she would go on without Don. What a grand time our group had visiting museums and eating. We were an eclectic group of fun-loving women with diverse interests. While some of the gals got together in the evenings for a hit of pot, Glorya and I curled up on a sofa, ate our white asparagus, and talked until the wee hours. While we all enjoyed the artistic pursuits, there were, of course, the proverbial shopping trips. On one such afternoon of window-shopping the streets of Paris, Glorya fell in love with a Piaget watch. Considering the modest price, it was a great find. I congratulated her on recognizing such a treasure and was surprised not at her hesitance to buy it but at the reason for her hesitance. She explained to me that Don would not approve or allow her to buy it. Of course I was shocked that at this point in her life she would have to get permission for such a purchase. Kaufman and Broad was an international company that Don and his partner Eli had built from the ground up, and it didn't take a Rhodes Scholar to figure out that they had money. When I suggested she just call and ask, she dismissed the idea on the grounds that he would just refuse. I watched her dilemma unfold and saw the personal turmoil she was putting herself through. She really wanted that watch, and I pointed out to her that the purchase of it was not going to cause any financial hardship for her family members. On the other hand, she wanted to do what she had done her entire marriage: be the good and dutiful wife. It's the age-old story of the sharing or not sharing of power and control in a relationship. Books, lives, and histories have been written on the subject. Glorya was truly perplexed. Over a cup of cappuccino at a sidewalk café, I finally made my point and convinced her to buy the watch. The irony of the purchase was that she used grocery money she had squirreled away to buy the watch.

Fast-forward to when Glorya arrived home from the Paris trip and told Don she had purchased the watch. His only comment was, "How much did it cost?" Trained well and so fearful of repercussions, she reduced the purchase price by half, and he still flipped out. This from a man with a garage full of every toy imaginable including seven motorcycles, seven Jaguars, a bi-wing airplane, and expensive ski equipment for helicopter skiing. It was certainly evident to me that Glorya was madly in love with Don. She had married when she was very young and impressionable. Twelve years her senior, Don was a street-smart man of the world who grew up attending the school of hard knocks and became a self-made millionaire before he turned forty. Glorya was like many women before the women's revolution: a wife under her husband's thumb because she was without a career of her own and without the ability to make her own money. It was evident when I was around the two of them that Don was also very much in love with Glorya, but his love hinged on her subservience. His word was law in the household, while Glorya didn't have a voice. This did absolutely nothing to promote the children's respect for their mother, and as a result she was not honored by them as a mother. The world ran on "Don Time," and it was virtually impossible for Glorya to manifest her individuality. He was a powerful man, and her speaking up for herself was virtually impossible.

When I think back to the sweet, funny, and warm young thing who sat with me in Paris eating white asparagus, scared to death to take a chance on buying a watch, I can't help but marvel at the woman that I still call my friend today. The obstacles she has overcome and her vast accomplishments are astounding to me, especially since she has done all of this without losing an ounce of the sweet, funny, warm girl who drew me into the wonderfulness of her friendship from the very first night we met. I love Glorya so much, and I am sad not only for the three of her children who have chosen to not be a part of her life, but for the many grandchildren and great-grandchildren who, because of their parents' choices, will never get to know the fabulous, caring woman who people all over the world, from all walks of life, have grown to love, respect, and admire.

**Curtis's bar mitzvah**

**Don Kaufman and Samson**

**The Kaufmans—Front row, L to R: Laura, Glorya, Eva and Sam Pinkis. Back row, L to R: Don, Stacie, Curt, Gayl**

**Glorya and Troy at Amber Hills**

**Glorya Kaufman and Deborah Schwartz**

# Laura

One of the heartbreaks of my life was my delightful, beautiful daughter Laura's diagnosis of schizophrenia. It was painful for me to watch Laura in *The Roaring Kaufmans* and see her so full of life and promise. This child who was my first, and whom I loved and still love so very much, was robbed of the life that Don and I wished and dreamed for all of our children. There is no greater pain for a mother than to see her child spiral to the depths and to have no recourse but to stand by helplessly witnessing the horrific event. Add to that the fact that she needed to live in a special home in order to receive care for her illness, and I was pretty much devastated. Laura went on to have a beautiful daughter April, who is still a light in my life. Her beautiful face and dark curly hair, accented by her adorable dimples, epitomize the spitfire that she has always been. When Laura, unmarried, became pregnant, I of course considered her illness and her limited abilities and was against her having the child. In the seventies it was bad enough to be pregnant and unmarried. In light of the diagnosis of schizophrenia, which is hereditary, I voiced my concerns about her having the baby. But I cannot imagine my life, or Laura's life without this delightful, intuitive breeze of a gal, and now April's son, Mario Maximus, is yet another blessing in my life.

Always a loving child and great student, Laura was in the ninety-eighth percentile of her class at Beverly Hills High School. Like her dad, she was also a great athlete. She skied beautifully and was a great swimmer. Ever the avid outdoorsman, Don wanted his children to enjoy all the activities he loved so much. He would take them scuba diving, white-water rafting, camping on horseback in the wilderness, and for exciting rides in his bi-wing plane where he thrilled them with aerobatic stunts. Two days before Laura was to leave for college in Northern California, Don decided to take the family for a hang-gliding adventure to a park called Escape Country. It was to be a celebration of the first child of the family going off to college, but it would become much more than that. It would prove to be a decision that would change the lives of every family member.

Except for Stacie, who was at a bar mitzvah, the family was game for the adventure. Everyone had a lesson in how to manage the hang glider. Unable to even lift the glider, I was just a spectator, but Don, Gayl, and Curtis all had exceptional flights, and they had a great time. Laura was the last to go, but as she took off from a small hill, the winds changed. A crosswind and a down-draft caught her glider, and she was blown to the next hill, which was much higher. She crash-landed from a twenty-foot drop, resulting in a fractured pelvis, a broken arm, and a concussion. She was rushed to the emergency room and came home a wounded young lady.

Laura was two weeks behind schedule leaving for college, and she missed the start of the semester with the other freshmen. Laura was never again the same girl we all knew and loved. She did not finish her first semester and came home delusional and unbalanced. We admitted her to a psychiatric hospital, where it was determined that she had experimented with LSD and other unspecified drugs and that she was schizophrenic. Our daughter's diagnosis and her need to live apart from us in a special facility broke our hearts. This was a huge heartbreak for Don, who had witnessed the same mental illness in his mother. It was so hard on the whole family.

# The Bike Accident

In 1978, our kids were pretty much on their own, and Don and I were once again beginning to have more time for just the two of us. We always enjoyed activities with friends, and it was not unusual for us to rent bikes and go for a ride, especially at the beach. But one particular outing, bike riding on the path in Hermosa Beach, would change my life.

The path changed to a decline with a sharp (ninety-degree) turn at the bottom of the hill. The pathway was treacherous, steep, and covered with sand, making it difficult to control the bicycle. I went into a skid and was thrown into a wall. Don and two friends had gotten ahead of me and had stopped to wait. Instead of me catching up to them, they got the police, who came to inform them of my accident.

The accident rendered me unconscious, with a concussion; multiple fractures to my left cheekbone (a displaced left-trimalar fracture), which required surgery; a cut over my left eyebrow, which required twenty stitches; and multiple bruises and abrasions. I was rushed to the Harbor Medical Center, now the Harbor-UCLA Medical Center, in Torrance.

Don rode with me in the ambulance to the hospital. What was interesting is that the nurse taking care of me in the hospital had seen my accident from her apartment window, which overlooked the bike path, and she would be a witness at the eventual trial. I knew Don was beside himself, but I didn't realize just how distraught he was until much later when my daughter Gayl told me that when Don called home, he was crying. Don never cried.

Immediately after the accident I had to have a nurse with me twenty-four hours a day due to the possibility of suffocation from the swelling. I was suffering a great deal of pain in my face, neck, and jaw, as the mandibular joints were pushed out of place. Eventually I had to wear braces to help correct my bite. In addition, all the teeth on both sides of my mouth had to be shaved down and replaced with porcelain crowns. I had headaches for about four years, and it also took that long to get back to normal eating patterns. It would take four years for my suit against Hermosa Beach to go to trial.

Beside recovering from extensive bodily injury, and beside the ordeal and stress of the trial, I was also going through intense emotional changes. The last four years of my marriage had been the best of the twenty-eight years we were married because of the attitude adjustment on Don's part. He was truly more caring, more tolerant, and dare I say, yes, more respectful of me, my feelings, and my opinions. I'm sorry it took an accident of such life-threatening proportions to give him a wake-up call. I believe he appreciated me in a way he never had, and perhaps he never realized what I meant to him until he almost lost me. I guess God felt desperate times called for desperate measures, because once the trial ended, I was destined to only have Don in my life for two more months. He must have been waiting for the trial to be over with and my injuries to be healed before he left me to care for myself—forever. God definitely works in mysterious and unexplainable ways.

## Norris Bishton: Attorney

For twenty-two miles along the Los Angeles oceanfront there is a paved bike path. The bike path passes through a number of municipalities. On Saturday September 30, 1978, Glorya Kaufman was riding southbound on her bicycle with her husband, Don, and two friends, when they came to the point where the bike path leaves the city of Manhattan Beach and enters the city of Hermosa Beach. Each city is responsible for the bike path within its borders. The two cities had a dispute as to how the sections of the bike path within each city should be joined at the border. What should have been a continuous path was instead a treacherous challenge requiring a bicyclist to navigate a steep, narrow ramp ending in a cement block wall, where the bicyclist had to make a ninety-degree left turn to continue. The design of the ramp caused it to be covered with blown sand, which accumulated in the turn area. No signs warned a bicyclist of the danger.

It was three in the afternoon when Glorya came upon the ramp and headed down. Halfway down she realized she was in trouble and attempted to brake her bicycle on the sand-covered ramp without success. She slammed into the cement block wall and was thrown from her bicycle. She suffered abrasions and bruises, but her most serious injury was to her jaw. She had seriously injured her temporomandibular joint.

I represented Glorya in a civil suit against the city of Hermosa Beach for injuries caused by a dangerous condition created by the negligence of the city and for maintaining a dangerous condition after having actual knowledge of the danger. As it turned out, Glorya was not the first person injured on the steep ramp, which was known as "accident wall" due to the multitude of accidents that had occurred there. My recollections are from my vantage point as Glorya's attorney.

I was aware the Kaufmans were well off, and I was curious why Glorya wanted to go through the ordeal of a lawsuit. I immediately determined that it was not about the money. Glorya rightly felt that the existing ramp provided for bicyclists was actually a menace. Throughout the lawsuit Glorya was equally upset about what had happened to her and the dangers the ramp presented to others. I felt that Glorya was a little frustrated with me because I lacked the power to somehow cause Hermosa Beach to immediately remedy the situation.

Lawsuits took forever to get to trial in the late 1970s and early 1980s. I had great difficulty getting Hermosa Beach to answer questions concerning the ramp and other accidents on the ramp. I had to go to court a number of times to get the judge to force Hermosa Beach to turn over records and answer questions. I had difficulty identifying anyone from the city who knew anything about the ramp or its maintenance. I recall that depositions of city employees were largely a waste of time.

Glorya's recollections of the accident were still vivid. By then I was aware that the city's defense would claim that the accident was Glorya's fault. Glorya was a little taken aback that anyone would suggest the accident was her fault.

There was a long lunch every day for Don, Glorya, my fiancé Debi, and me. We would discuss whatever we had to discuss about the trial and then a wide range of topics. We might have tried the courthouse cafeteria food once. What I remember is we found a nondescript restaurant nearby where we could have some privacy, and we went back to the same place each day. I do not remember any tension at the lunches. If anyone can have fun during a jury trial, we had fun during the lunches. Don told stories, we discussed the trials and tribulations of having children (I had three sons from an earlier marriage and was raising them as a single father), and we discussed world affairs.

The jury deliberated for two days and part of a third day. On October 18, the jury returned a verdict. My recollection is that Glorya and Don were in the courtroom for the verdict. Glorya was awarded a settlement, and she later told me that she used the money to open her first checking account. But the bigger win was her reason for bringing the lawsuit. Hermosa Beach had to completely rework the bike path transition from Manhattan Beach. After the jury was released, my recollection is that we talked to some of the jurors and thanked them. Glorya and Don were most gracious, but the attorney for the city was quite upset. First, he brought a motion for judgment "notwithstanding" the verdict, which the judge denied on November 11. Then he filed a notice of appeal on December 3. Later in the month he finally gave up, and the judgment was paid.

Sometime in December, Glorya and Don invited me over to dinner. Going through a jury trial is like going through a war, and of course there are many war stories. We had a wonderful dinner going over the experience of the trial. I particularly remember the conversation about the upcoming visit of their pregnant daughter and her new husband from Israel. They were looking forward to their first grandchild. Just weeks later, tragedy struck. When I heard the news that Don had been killed, the first thing that occurred to me was how Don had insisted throughout the lawsuit that Glorya make the decisions—Almost as if he were fine-tuning her for what would be nothing but decision-making for many, many years to come. I saw her transform before my very eyes, so I had no doubt that Glorya would rise to the challenge and emerge victorious.

# Fate Steps In

I WAS CERTAINLY HAPPY THAT clear and sunny California morning. Don and I had just come home a few days earlier from a lovely Palm Springs adventure. Our wedding anniversary was December 26, and we always enjoyed a festive week together between our anniversary and New Year's. Often it would include skiing with the children, but this year it was just the two of us visiting our friends, Norman and Cecile Krevoy, and it was such fun. On the drive home toward Los Angeles, we passed a truck filled with white ducks and geese, and Don waved the driver to pull over. We asked where the ducks were headed and the driver said, "A Chinese restaurant." There was no way we were going to allow those ducks to become menu items, not when we had a beautiful lake on our forty-eight acres of property in the heart of Brentwood, crying out for more ducks. Some money changed hands, and the next thing I knew, Don and I were no longer alone in the car. The back seat was full of ducks and unfriendly geese!

I watched the beautiful ducks swimming peacefully along the lake and loving their new home. I was so happy for them as they quacked noisily. They had no idea of the fate they had narrowly escaped, just as I had no idea of our fate, which was only days away.

For the last twenty years, my husband had been around on a daily basis. As I've mentioned, at forty years old, Don had decided that he had made enough money, and he took an early retirement to enjoy sports and the family. On this day, our son Curtis had been home for several weeks on Christmas break from UC–San Diego, and our daughter Gayl and her husband Eyal had come in from Israel for the holidays and for Gayl's baby to be born in the United States. Gayl was seven months pregnant, and we were all so excited about the first Kaufman grandchild. That morning I prepared breakfast for Don, Curtis, and myself, and we all sat at the breakfast bar in the kitchen for a meeting that Curtis had called. Don, who always had young friends, was helping out with a few of Curtis's pals who were working out of their garage in Encino, creating an educational software program for children. Curtis was trying to convince Don to let him drop out of college to join the business.

Several things were very important and impactful to me about this family meeting over breakfast. First of all, Don instructed me that I was not to speak at the meeting. This was not unusual; I was never asked my opinion, so I learned not to give it. Because Don was retired, he was with us all the time, and his very big personality and management style dominated the family scene. My role was quite secondary and, having grown up with a domineering mother, I was accepting of this, perhaps more than I should have been.

Don told Curtis that he had to make his decision himself; that he was not going to tell him whether or not to drop out of school to pursue this business. What he was telling him was that if he in fact did drop out, he must go back later and finish his college education. This was crystal clear, and Curtis agreed to this bargain.[3]

After the meeting in the kitchen was adjourned, the next order of business for the day was Don and Eyal. Eyal had come to a crossroads in his life. He was just out of the Israeli army and not quite sure what he wanted to do. But now with a wife and baby on the way, he had to make some decisions fast and really needed guidance. Just a few days after the accident, on January 8, I found some jottings on Don's side of the partners desk that we had shared in the study. Given the content, it seems they were notes on how he would motivate Eyal to find direction in his life.

The first jotting was "Motivational Patterns: 1. Where do you want to go? 2. Trust to understand it. 3. Start going for it. Decide where you want to work, i.e., environment. Two big blocks: Time and Money. A. Do not be afraid to

---

3 Curtis ended up dropping out of school and in fact did make some money on the software venture. But he never honored his father's last request.

fail…failing is a learning process. B. Be alert to everything…confidence level high…you deserve it." The second jotting was, "Have faith in yourself; don't get intimidated. Believe in yourself, and go for it. Design what you want in the future." The third jotting was, "Who am I…what do I want to do…how do I do it? Set goals…make and give yourself specific time. Don't be afraid; feel you can do it."

I think these first jottings were Don's preparation for his time that he was going to spend with Eyal on that fateful day. And I am sure they discussed it over lunch. Many years later I shared these notes with my grandson Donald Tyler, Stacie's son, in the hopes that it would motivate him with his career choices.

Though it is bittersweet, I have come to believe that Don's last jotting, unbeknown to him, was a sort of going-away message to me: "Life is a journey, not a destination. Make each day part of the voyage. Create your own voyage. Enjoy each part of it." Create a voyage? Would I be able to do that? Was Don telling me how to carry on without him? Would I be able to journey on—and enjoy it?

Don said, "I want to take you for a ride in my plane." Don loved that plane and flew whenever he could make the time. Flying was his passion. I didn't think anything of it. Don had always told me that as long as he had on his parachute, he would be safe. As Gayl and I walked our husbands out to the front yard to see them off, everything was peaceful and in order. We waved good-bye, happy that the boys were off together for an adventure.

At about 4:00 p.m., Gayl was napping in the guesthouse, and I was in the kitchen with Curtis when the phone from the front gate rang. It was the police. I told them that I had not put in a call for the police, that everything was fine, and that there was no need for them to come in. They said they had to see me. I don't know even to this day if my resistance to them coming in was because I sensed something ominous. Perhaps I thought if I refused to admit them to the property, nothing could be wrong. Then they asked a question that made my vision narrow, and my heart all but stopped: "Does your husband own a bi-wing airplane?" Time stood still, and all I could hear was my heartbeat pounding in my ears. I felt my throat tighten. For a moment I wondered if I was in the middle of a horrible nightmare and might wake up at any moment.

The fact is that it was a horrible nightmare, but there would be no waking up from it—no having my husband next to me in the bed as I shared with him my awful nightmare, no one comforting me and assuring me that it was all just a bad dream. It was all horrifically real, and I was about to go through that nightmare alone. It's funny, but the only person on whom I truly could have leaned through all of this, the only person who had taken care of everything for me for the past twenty-eight years, was the only person who could not be there for me: Don. I don't remember admitting them through the gate, but my finger must have pressed the button because the next thing I knew, two uniformed policemen pulled up the driveway.

I watched the police officers get out of their patrol car and walk toward me. It was all in slow motion, and my heart was pounding. All I could think was, *When will they smile*? There were no smiles. They looked sober as I led them into the living room where Gayl and Curtis had come to see what all the commotion was about. Curtis was already on edge because he was in the kitchen with me when the police rang at the gate. But Gayl had just awakened from her nap when she saw the patrol car pull up. I stared at them while one of the officers gave us the most devastating news imaginable.

Don's bi-wing plane had crashed near Calabasas, and both he and Eyal were killed. Along with flying, one of Don's biggest passions in life was practical joking. In my mind, I kept screaming, *No, this isn't happening*! I then assured myself that he was going to walk in the door any minute, with his booming voice and infectious laughter. I told the officers I didn't believe them. Evidently Curtis and Gayl both did because all I could hear was Curtis screaming. He had dropped to the floor, screaming, and Gayl had fainted. Before I had another moment to try to grasp any part of what was happening, our friends Frank Bereny and his wife, Barbara, along with another couple, Dr. Seth Weingarten and his wife, Lyn Goldman, were all in the living room next to me. I was in total denial and still wouldn't accept what I was being told.

Frank had called twice earlier because he had heard on the radio that a bi-wing plane had crashed and that there were no survivors. He feared it might be Don, and he said that when I had told him that Don was out flying, he knew what had happened and rushed to the house with a physician. Thank God they arrived when they did. They called for an ambulance to rush Gayl to the hospital, fearing her emotional distress could cause her to lose the baby. Curtis was still wailing, and I was still in a state of shock, still telling the police that I didn't believe them. One of the officers placed something in my hand: my husband's wedding ring. Along with a phone call from the city morgue verifying the identities of the crash victims, I was left with no other choice than to believe what I was being told, that my husband and Gayl's husband were both dead. My grandfather clock, which Don wound weekly, had stopped that day at 2:30 p.m., just about the time of the crash—the time my husband took his last breath.

The official investigation concluded that no alcohol or drugs were found in either body. It also concluded that the plane developed mechanical problems shortly after takeoff from Santa Paula where Don and Eyal had stopped for lunch. Rendered uncontrollable, it plummeted straight down over Calabasas, crashed in a field, and burst into flames. The parachutes they both had on were useless, as they could not get out in time to use them. I don't know what was going through Don's mind in those last seconds when he must have known that even a Plan B wasn't going to save them. Eyal's body was thrown clear of the plane, which leads me to believe Don may have tried in some way to get Eyal out of the plane so that he could activate his parachute. I truly believe that was probably my husband's last thought: *How do I save this boy?*

The house was a blur of people that evening. The funeral was a blur; life was a blur. I was in a daze and truly don't remember a great deal about what was happening. I had lost the rock I had been anchored to for twenty-eight years. At a very young age, I had gone straight from my parents' home to being Don's wife. Don was a sophisticated man of the world when I married him and truly knew how to fend for himself. I, on the other hand, was a babe in arms. Don had kept me so sheltered, safe, and taken care of that I was, in a sense, his fifth child. Now, without any preparation or warning, I was left alone. I didn't know anything about our finances or assets and could only hope that I could find honest people to help me. My survival skills were nil! I could barely get myself out of bed every morning. I wasn't eating, and I quite quickly lost fifteen pounds. Dr. Herbert Singer, a friend of the family, finally gave me orders—not suggestions but orders. He said, "Glorya, you have to eat three meals a day—at eight a.m., noon, and six p.m." Like a child, I agreed with him that I had to do just that. I wasn't certain I could even do that. The one thing I knew with certainty was that nothing would ever be the same again—not for me and not for my children.

Right after the funeral, Curtis wanted to move into the house with his girlfriend and take over as the "man of the house." I nixed that immediately. After crying daily for months, and after the birth of her baby, Gayl went back to Israel, where she felt people coped in a much better way with loss. Stacie went back to her apartment, and Laura went back to the residential home. I was alone for the first time in my life.

After Don's death I worked for many years to honor him by opening a library in Brentwood in his name. The children all attended the library opening.

I had gone from being part of a family of six to being on my own—table for one. I was beginning to feel like one of the orphaned children I had dreamed of taking care of when I was a child. I was left like a marionette with its strings freshly cut. So much changed. If only I had known then what I learned many years later, I wouldn't have been so resistant and afraid of the changes. The philosopher Alan Watts said, "The only way to make sense of change is to plunge into it, move with it, and join the dance." And that is just what I did.

## Deborah Schwartz

My memory is clear on so many details, but I cannot remember how my mother told me that Mr. Kaufman and Eyal had been killed in a plane crash. After she told me, my mom dropped me off at the ranch, and I went in through the kitchen and made my way to the living room where Mrs. Kaufman sat on the couch, surrounded by many people. She looked up, and our eyes met.

"I just wanted you to know I was here," I said. She reached out to me, the crowd parted, and I fell into her arms. For thirty-three years I have carried in my heart not only what she said but how she said it, a simple sentence filled with painful emotion, "Oh, Debbie, he loved you so much." It was just what I needed to hear.

With heavy hearts, each of us picked up the pieces and got on with life. Gayl moved to Israel, had her baby, and eventually married Eyal's best friend. Laura went back to her residential home, Stacie returned to her apartment, Curt and his girlfriend, Jill, moved in together, and I settled in Calabasas with my boyfriend.

That left Mrs. Kaufman by herself at the ranch. I wouldn't know what she dealt with after her husband's death until many years later. Mrs. Kaufman, who had gone from her parents' home to marrying Don and being a wife and mother for twenty-eight years, was left to reinvent herself and survive.

# Interlude and Remembrance

I HAVE LOVED TWO MEN in my life, Don and my dad, and I was fortunate that they also loved each other. Dad loved Don so much that he was never the same after Don's death. They had such fun playing snooker at the house, and Dad always felt like he had lost his only son.

After Don's tragic death my life changed forever. I began the slow process of reinventing myself and creating the life I have today. The two final sections of this book will describe that journey.

At this point in the narrative I would like to share the words of a few dear friends who have known me most of my life—before, during and after my marriage to Don.

# Friends

## Reza Neghabat: Husband of My Friend Harriette

Sometime in the autumn of 1983, a serene and beautiful woman came into my life. I will forever hold her as my guiding angel. A gathering of architects were to be briefed by her for the library project honoring her deceased husband. I was only there to accompany and assist my architect friend with translating English. Glorya's calm, professional, and classy presentation was so exceptional that I had no choice but to introduce myself to her and offer my congratulations. Even though I felt the aura of sadness that enveloped her from the recent loss of her husband, her genuine kindness and intelligence was a shining light that could not be missed. Soon we were sharing stories of our trips to France and all the interesting people and places we had discovered. I left the meeting that day knowing that somehow and in some way we were going to remain friends.

I was born and raised in Iran, and after many years of traveling all over the place, settling in Los Angeles was in the back of my mind when I met Glorya that fateful day. I do say "fateful," because this woman changed the course of my life, which is I why I call her my guiding angel. A month or so after our first meeting, Glorya introduced me to her friend Harriette, who eventually agreed to become my wife. She has been my fair lady for the past thirty-three years. Our very special and dear friend Glorya is still our angel. I cannot come close to expressing my love for and appreciation of Glorya, not just for introducing me to my wife but also for being a citizen of the world. What Glorya is doing for all of humanity in so many areas is a tribute to her tireless efforts to make the world a better place. I am blessed and honored that the place she will always occupy for me in my heart is that of my angel.

## Harriette Craig-Neghabat: A Friend

My neighbors across the street, Don and Glorya Kaufman, lived about three miles from my ranch home; those three miles were the combination of our long and winding driveways! We were new neighbors as my husband, Ken Roberts, and I had just moved into our ranch home. Shortly after settling in, I was visited by Laura Kaufman, the oldest of the four Kaufman children, bearing cookies and a bright smile. Even though Ken and I did not have children, and Don and Glorya spent all of their time with their brood, we still managed to get together for an occasional dinner at one of our homes. Glorya and I had personal interests in common, and I soon found myself introduced by her at charity events, sightseeing trips, art exhibits, and other pleasant gatherings. She really took me under her wing.

After a bike accident in 1978 left her with serious injuries requiring extensive surgeries, I spent more time visiting her at her home, bringing her special foods, and, when she was able, taking walks along the canyon to ease her distress. Our friendship grew to a deeper level of two women facing various obstacles.

Sometime after Glorya's husband's death, my marriage to Ken ended in divorce, but he and I managed to remain friends, and Ken, Glorya, and I attended parties and shared Thanksgiving dinners and Christmas gatherings for many years. Glorya was coming into her own, and whereas before she had been fearful, she came to enjoy traveling and discovering new places! She even had the courage to go alone! Soon after Don's death, Glorya and I planned a trip to Europe together. It would be an opportunity for Glorya and I to leave some of our difficult experiences behind us for a short time. Glorya had become thin during her months of mourning and had lost about fifteen pounds from an already slim figure. Her clothes were loose, and we got a giggle out of the fact that she had to keep stopping to pull up her socks or knee-high stockings. We both agreed that for whatever reason, it felt good to laugh.

We traveled through many cities in Italy, enjoying the art galleries, jewelry, sunshine, and the excellent food. We then traveled to Paris for the beauty and delight of the city. It was here that Glorya fell in love with Paris and all of its splendor. She would come to travel to Paris on a regular basis, with friends or alone. If she traveled alone, which she often did, she felt fine because the city was always her "date."

It was about this same time that Glorya planned and initiated the Donald Bruce Kaufman Library in honor and in memory of her husband. Glorya introduced me to Reza Neghabat, a gentleman she had met while working with the city officials in Brentwood. Glorya has a keen sense of personalities, and she was certainly right about this pairing. Reza and I fell in love and got married. Over the thirty-plus years that we have been married, Glorya has joined us at special events, including the marriages of both of our children. Whatever she was going through in her own life, Glorya never faltered as a mainstay of emotional support, friendship, and love for our family.

Glorya has funded many forward-thinking projects for various medical needs in our community, women's programs, and children's clinics. Through these endeavors, she has learned the ups and downs of international philanthropy and business, gaining an invaluable education while bettering her community by supporting the arts and addressing societal and educational needs. She always did her homework. Researching dance and performance criteria in many cities of the United States and Europe, and with guidance from professionals in the dance field, she absorbed facts and details of dance production and the structure required for dancers to live, learn, and work. Her eagerness to advance and improve the performing arts made it exciting just to be around her. It still is today. That little Energizer Bunny of Glorya Kaufman never quits!

## Deborah Schwartz

After Mr. Kaufman's death I was busy raising a family and did not see Glorya for some time. We renewed our friendship after many years at a family event. It was wonderful to see her again and sit together with her after the years that had passed. She told me all about the library branch she had built in Brentwood to honor Mr. Kaufman after his death. He loved reading very much, and the library was quite a labor of love. It took eleven years to complete the project.

We hiked every nook and cranny of the ranch, and we examined every new flower and rosebush she had planted, but I was not prepared for the incredible transformation of the grounds and main house at Glorya's artistic hand. I knew she was a fabulous painter; I found that her artistic gift extended to what she had done with every aspect of the ranch. The ranch grounds now looked like a colorful, splashy painting. There wasn't an inch of property that wasn't tended and manicured. And this place I loved so much, that held so many wonderful memories for me, also had a new name: Amber Hills. Glorya had placed sculptures throughout the grounds. Some were colorful and whimsical, and others were contemporary. They were all a celebration of life. As we toured the redecorated house, I couldn't get over how much I loved everything she had done. From her Erté statues to her fabulous sculpted glass coffee tables and Lalique vases, everything was beautiful and reflected her aura. An entire new wing had been added to the downstairs past the library. It was Glorya's new master suite, and it was fabulous. It began with a beautiful glass door of two tango dancers, designed and made especially for her. The backyard wrapped around the room, allowing a gorgeous view of the mountains.

The window in a bathroom was especially designed in frosted glass with etched bubbles, one of Glorya's favorite things. She told me how much she loved bubbles and fireworks, that you just have to enjoy them while they are in front of your eyes—like life. We had lunch on the newly screened-in patio that looked out to the yard and the beautiful oak trees and mountains. My senses flooded with memories. Now a flag waved in the breeze as if protecting the grounds and holding our memories safe.

Years later, when Glorya decided to have the barn demolished because it was falling apart, she wanted my blessing that it was OK. We walked the grounds for an entire day while my husband Doug took pictures of us in every conceivable spot, with every possible pose and background. I made her a beautiful photo album with at least two hundred pictures. There was a time for the ranch, and that time had come to an end. Now it was time for a change. It was actually time for some freedom and a new home in the heart of Beverly Hills. It would soon be time for her new home: Chateau de Liberté.

As we strolled the grounds of the ranch together, the sunlight lit up her still-beautiful red hair, and I marveled that she was even more beautiful than I remembered. Her trim figure was adorned in the most stylish outfit, and since over the years my interest had shifted from horses to being a "clothes horse," we were destined to have great fun shopping—only not at Loehmann's. Our shopping afternoons always ended with an iced vanilla coffee at our favorite coffee shop, Comoncy, on Bedford Drive, where we kept chatting up a storm, even after we had been together for hours.

There were so many wonderful things that Glorya was now doing with her time, and I just knew how proud Mr. Kaufman would have been of her accomplishments. Let's face it: There is a multitude of wealthy widows who do nothing but shop, go to lunch, and have plastic surgery. Glorya was making contributions in many arenas, but mostly she was making a name for herself as a dance philanthropist. In Glorya's words, "Dance and music are an international language. With it, we can touch everyone." There is a reason Glorya is referred to as the Duchess of Dance.

I have Glorya to thank for turning me on to the arts in so many media that I would not have pursued myself. On a grander scale, this is what she is doing for the entirety of the country, not to mention the world: exposing people of all ages to dance and the arts that they may not have ever dreamed they would love and enjoy.

I have had the good fortune to have known Glorya for most of my life, and it goes without saying that a Glorya-less world is impossible for me to imagine, so I won't. I have seen her in the depths of despair and sadness, and I have seen her at the height of success and happiness. She has never taken her life for granted or felt in any way superior to others. Her first reaction to a difficult situation is to try to figure out what she can do to help, whether it be for just one person who is suffering or for a community. One of the things I find the most commendable about Glorya and her many donations is that even though the dollar amounts surface from other sources, she herself does not advertise them. This is not the part she wants remembered. Her work is her legacy.

If I have a tendency to toot Glorya's horn, it is with good and valid reason: I feel it is in order. If there is one wish that I have for the woman who began to care for others by saving her pennies in her mother's tzedakah box and proceeded to help the disadvantaged and to become the Duchess of Dance, it is for her to know, to really know, not just how much she has contributed or the countless lives she has touched and changed, but also how much she is loved.

PART 3

# Starting Over

# Time to Take Stock

The moment in between who you once were and who you are now becoming is where the dance of life really takes place.

—Barbara de Angelis

I remember standing in front of a mirror and taking a long, hard, critical look at myself. I told myself, *It's either sink or swim*. It was the first step in the right direction: deciding what changes I wanted to make and taking stock of my weaknesses. I knew I wanted to reinvent myself. I also knew it was time to stop counting my troubles and start calculating my happiness; I just hadn't a clue as to how. Could it really be as simple as Abraham Lincoln said: "Folks are usually about as happy as they make up their minds to be"? I had to seriously consider this.

I wanted to become a different person, and that began with thinking about others who were far worse off than me. I tapped into the lesson that both of my parents had taught me: that I should share with others less fortunate. I remembered the little blue and white tzedakah boxes in the window of our home where we had collected pennies and nickels. I remembered the feeling of pride and happiness I experienced at being able to put even the smallest amount of change into the little tzedakah, because I knew it was to help others.

I decided that my mother's legacy would be the model for my own life. I knew I wanted to help others and make a difference, maybe not by building an orphanage but in some meaningful way.

For as long as I can remember, my parents loved to dance, and I learned this love of dance from them. I knew I had to factor creativity, and, yes, fun, back into my life. During my teen years, my sense of humor was keen, and I dated, danced, and laughed.

I forced myself to begin making my own decisions at every turn in order to take control of my own life. I fired all the brokers, electricians, and plumbers who told me to do things the way Don would like them done. I was determined to value myself, and I was going to fight for my independence in what I saw as a man's world. I wanted to take control over the direction my life would take.

Part of what draws me to the marionette painting in my office is that he is in a yoga pose. I practiced yoga before and after Don's death, and it motivated me to get out of bed in the morning. I think yoga saved my life. It gave me strength, and, oh boy, was I going to need it.

As I've mentioned, Don had left his business partner, Eli Broad, as the special trustee of our estate. Eli now had enormous power over me and my family. He was in charge of all the funds in my estate, and I had no say; I couldn't make a move without his approval. I determined that I had to fight for my independence, a battle that would last for the next thirty-two years.

Don had set up three trusts. The first, a marital trust, is for the benefit of the surviving spouse. Assets are moved into the trust, and the income generated by the assets goes to the surviving spouse. When the spouse dies, the trust passes to the heirs. The second, a survivor's trust, also for the benefit of the surviving spouse, also contains personal property. I could not make decisions or investments with the money; I could only spend it. The third trust, an exemption trust for the children, was set up to drastically reduce taxes. Eli, as special trustee, had the primary fiduciary duty to me and my children.

I did a great deal for all my children with the survivor's trust. After her second marriage, I bought and furnished a house for my daughter Gayl and her family in Israel. I also bought her a home in Los Angeles so her children could go to school and learn to speak English when they were young, so that they wouldn't speak with an accent. Stacie moved to Paris, and I bought her a lovely apartment as she was expecting her first child. I bought Laura a house in Encino, and I was thrilled that she was doing well enough to handle her own home. Curtis was already married and living in northern California. I gave him a substantial amount of cash and told him to use it for investments since he already owned a home.

I had an excellent and well-respected attorney and CPA, Nathan Schwartz. He would visit me once a month and explain my portfolios. He told me one of the accounts was churning and losing a great deal of income. Eli was the only one who could make a change, and he was very slow to respond to my requests. I wanted to handle my own estate. At last that day arrived: In 2014, after thirty years of frustration, I was free from the marital trust and the survivor's trust.

The marionette painting in my office is a daily reminder that I ultimately won this battle. No one will ever pull my strings again.

## Luan Phan: Attorney

During 2012 and 2013, Glorya showed her true strength when she was attacked in a $100 million lawsuit filed against her by Eli Broad. The lawsuit arose out of a complicated estate plan set up by Don and Glorya many years before. Under Don and Glorya's estate plan, upon Don's death, two trusts for Glorya's benefit were established, one called the survivor's trust (which was funded with Glorya's portion of the family estate) and the other called the marital trust (which was funded out of Donald's portion of the family estate). The marital trust was much larger than the survivor's trust. Glorya was entitled to all the net income from both trusts during her lifetime. On her death, the property of the survivor's trust was to be distributed as Glorya directed, and the property of the marital trust was to be distributed to Glorya's children.

For many years following Donald's death in 1983, the average annual income earned by the marital trust was about 1.6 percent, which was about 70 percent below the industry standard of 5 percent. The poor income performance of the marital trust resulted in a significant part from its investments being heavily concentrated in growth stock, which the special trustee did not want to sell because the sale would result in large capital-gains taxes. This investment strategy was good for Glorya's children, the remainder beneficiaries of the marital trust who were enjoying the benefit of the appreciation, but not for Glorya, the lifetime beneficiary who was receiving the income.

Glorya asked the administrative trustee (J. P. Morgan Chase Bank N.A.) and the then–special trustee (Edward Landry) to address this situation, which violated her right to a reasonable income from the trust.[4] Finally, in early 1995, J. P. Morgan and Landry filed a petition jointly requesting the court to approve a modification of the way in which Glorya's income distributions from the marital trust would be calculated. They proposed a formula that benefitted Glorya in that she would receive a reasonable annual distribution that would be funded from income to the extent available and from principal to the extent income was insufficient. It also benefitted Glorya's children, who would be able to continue enjoying the appreciation of the marital trust's overconcentration in growth stock.

The new formula, proposed by Glorya, set her annual income distribution at the greater of the actual trust income or 3 percent of the value of the trust principal. Glorya could have asked for and received 5 percent since that was the average annual return for a trust like the marital trust at the time. However, in a spirit of compromise and goodwill, she chose not to do so.

In May 1995, the court approved that petition and made an order approving the new distribution-calculation method the trustees had proposed. For the next eighteen years, Glorya's annual distributions from the marital trust were made on the basis of the 1995 court order. No one ever complained or contended that the income payments made to Glorya were inaccurate or inappropriate during those years.

However, in July 2012, Edward Landry resigned as special trustee and Eli Broad surprisingly stepped back in as special trustee. In November 2012, Broad filed a lawsuit against Glorya in an attempt to drastically reduce her

---

4 From 1983 until 1995 Eli Broad served as special trustee. In 1995 Broad appointed Edward Landry to the position. Landry served as special trustee until July of 2012.

annual distributions from the marital trust and require her to reimburse all the principal distributions made to her from the marital trust under the 1995 court order, plus interest. Broad's lawsuit demanded over $100 million from Glorya. Neither J. P. Morgan nor Broad contacted Glorya or her advisors to discuss the matter before Broad filed his lawsuit. Broad timed the filing of his lawsuit to coincide with a large banquet that USC had scheduled to honor Glorya for her generous donation to found USC's new School of Dance.

Glorya vigorously opposed Broad's lawsuit, especially the reimbursement claim, which she viewed as meritless and having been filed in bad faith because Landry and J. P. Morgan, who were both appointed by Broad, had jointly filed the petition resulting in the 1995 court order. For eighteen years Landry and J. P. Morgan had followed that distribution order, and no one had raised any objections.

Glorya demanded a meeting with Broad to question him about the lawsuit. At that meeting, Glorya and I as her attorney, specifically asked Broad how he could sue Glorya given that all the payments had been determined and made by Landry and J. P. Morgan pursuant to a court order. Broad essentially contended that Landry and J. P. Morgan had mistakenly overpaid Glorya for eighteen years. Glorya and her attorney then asked why Broad had not sued Landry and J. P. Morgan, since they were the ones in charge and responsible for making the payments. If any mistakes had been made, Landry and J. P. Morgan were the ones who made them, not Glorya, who was merely an innocent income beneficiary. Broad appeared uncomfortable and did not offer an explanation before his attorney intervened to cut off the questioning. After the meeting ended, Glorya was quite giddy as she surmised that the great and powerful Eli Broad was probably not used to having a woman stand up to him. If Eli Broad honestly believed that mistakes had been made in the distributions to Glorya, why did he not sue the ones responsible for making those mistakes? Why did he choose to only sue Glorya, when she did not make the determinations or the distributions?

In August 2014, the case was settled, and Glorya felt completely vindicated. With respect to the claims made against her by Eli Broad, Glorya did not have to reimburse the trust for any of the payments she received in the past eighteen years. And, under the settlement, her annual distributions from the marital trust continued to be calculated in the manner approved by the 1995 court order. Furthermore, she was able to force Eli Broad to resign as special trustee from her trust and also to make J. P. Morgan resign as administrative trustee. Glorya replaced them with Wilbank Roche and Harvey Bookstein, respectively.

# Life after Don

My life spiraled in so many directions after Don's death. It was a pick-a-direction-and-deal-with-it kind of existence on a daily basis. And I do say *existence* deliberately; the first year was a fog, and I was dazed and still in shock. Every single thing reminded me of him, and everything was hard to do. It was very hard to get rid of his clothing. But it was even harder to get rid of his cars.

Don had seven Jaguars, but they all had Chevy engines. He had his mechanic, a burly bear of a guy, switch out all the Jaguar motors and replace them with Chevrolet parts so that the cars wouldn't break down. His silver Jaguar had a license plate that read ZYGAZUNT, which is a Hebrew word for "good health." It was auctioned off for more money than it was worth because of the license plate. But it was the red, sporty Jaguar convertible that was the hardest for me to let go of; to me it meant letting *him* go and facing the fact that he wasn't coming back—ever again. I had donated our RV to Big Brothers, and I donated Don's rifles to the Gene Autry Museum, but Curtis decided he wanted the RV and the rifles. After he spoke to both charities, they were both afraid of a lawsuit and declined the donations. It was hard to let go of anything, but I was learning that growth would only come from letting go.

One of the lessons I learned during this trying period was that goals set forth did not necessarily come to fruition in the time allowed. I found this a frustrating and difficult lesson to learn. I found that, faced with great adversity, my only hope was to persevere; I learned that if opportunities did not present themselves right away or on my time schedule, I could not give up. I also learned a great lesson from the dear, late Milton Berle, whose advice was, "If opportunity doesn't knock, build a door." How important this advice would become in my later philanthropic endeavors!

For the time being I knew with certainty that I had to keep going. No, I didn't know it—I chose it. I chose to move forward. I decided right then and there that I would strive to accept only two choices for myself: winning and learning. I could no longer compromise just to please others.

The kids were all having a very hard time, so I had a psychologist come to the house for me and the kids to try to deal with the loss of our leader. When a parent dies prematurely, it is easy for the children to elevate the dead parent to the position of being able to do no wrong. When Don died, the children put their father on a pedestal, and there he stayed. Meanwhile, in my children's eyes, I was a mere mortal capable of only making mistakes and causing them further pain. The kids didn't want to come together to heal. They preferred to run to their respective corners to lick their wounds—and there they have stayed.

# Choices and Ordeals

I HAVE ALWAYS BEEN FORTUNATE to have good friends. After Don died, I dated frequently, through introductions from friends or meeting someone attractive and interesting. I have to laugh at the fact that when I dated as a teen, I eventually met my date's parents. Now, I was being introduced to my date's children. I had more than my share of interesting male friends; however, I never fell in love with any of them. I might have missed a great opportunity, but that was not in my cards. For the first time in my life, I did not have an obligation to anyone but myself, and I wanted to explore that foreign territory. It was time for my choices—time for me to make a plan for myself.

I had one very special friend for over twenty years that I met at a party, and his name was Yves de Saint Laurent. He was not the dress designer, but he was French. He had retired and was living in an exquisite home in Bel Air that he allowed me to redesign and furnish for him. He was so easy to work with, and he had wonderful art pieces that he collected from all over the world. The evening I met him we had a lovely conversation, and he walked me to my car and said good night. The next day I received three dozen long-stemmed French pink roses. I did not know who they were from until several days later when Yves called me from Paris and asked if I had received his flowers. When he returned from Europe, our friendship started. Yves was the most generous gentleman I have ever known, which was new to me. He was always ready to treat whomever we were with to dinner. I once told him to let others pick up the check, as he never considered that an option. Our politics were not the same, so we did not discuss them. On occasion, with friends, the conversations turned to politics, and Yves was extremely strong and opinionated. I did not want to get in an argument with him.

I have no proof, but it is my opinion that he worked for the CIA. He would leave on sudden trips at times when there was trouble in another part of the world. When he returned, he told me he was in a government plane and had to lie down during the entire flight because there were no seats. That was my clue. I never asked him, because I knew if he wanted me to know what he was doing, he would tell me. He took me on a most fantastic trip; we drove to the south of France and saw his family estate in Normandy where his family had hidden Jews from the Nazis. I met his two brothers and their families. They were quite an illustrious family. Yves had been knighted by the queen of England. He showed me his many medals. I recall he was also a viscount and that he received the OBE (Order of the British Empire). I truly do not know all the honors that were bestowed on him. As we drove through Europe, he showed me the family's different homes while telling me stories about designers that would come to the house and fit him and his brothers for clothes. The three boys were cared for by a nanny, and they traveled with large suitcases filled with their new wardrobes when they went to their summer home. Just hearing his stories was like reading a novel about the privileged in Europe. His father was a duke and was given land on the Saint Laurent River, and that's how he got his last name. Yves and I remained friends until he died in Paris from complications of diabetes. I will always cherish our time together and the memories of the many wonderful experiences he afforded me.

# St. Moritz

I DECIDED I NEEDED A diversion—an escape. I needed something I had never done before, an adventurous trip on my own. I always wanted to ski in St. Moritz. I had never been alone at a resort or gone skiing alone. I was truly going to reinvent myself.

For fifteen years the Kaufman family had spent every year skiing in Aspen between Christmas and New Year's. On the nineteen-hour drive to Aspen Square, we would take turns at the wheel of our GMC recreational vehicle, which slept six. Before we left, I would cook a turkey and a brisket, which would be devoured by the family over the holiday. There was a city market across the street, so I would shop daily for veggies and fruit to enhance the meals. We often invited people we skied with to be guests for dinner, and the family would happily discuss their adventures from the day.

With that in mind, the year after Don died, I decided to go to Switzerland and stay in St. Moritz at the famous Palace Hotel for a week of skiing. I had seen the Palace Hotel in several films, and it was something I wanted to experience. So this would be the beginning of the many changes I would make. The idea that I had never gone to a resort alone, or skied alone, didn't concern me greatly.

The hotel is called the Palace, now Badrutt's Palace Hotel, for a very good reason. Every inch of it, inside and out, is palatial. The first evening, the guests were invited for a reception and orientation. I met Elizabeth Juen, a lovely young Austrian woman who had a real-estate business in Austin, Texas. We immediately became friends. She was an excellent skier and actually had been a ski instructor in Vail before moving to Austin. She skied the most difficult slopes with an expert instructor, while I signed up with an instructor who would guide me through the mountains that I could handle. We would meet at the day's end and share our adventures over dinner. We would then go dancing at various hotels. What seems to stick with me most is how much laughing we did. There was a day that we decided we would go on a snowshoe expedition. It was very hard to trudge through the snow wearing tennis rackets for shoes. My feet got tangled, and down I went. Elizabeth, in her quest to save me and also laughing hysterically, got herself in a tangle, and down she went. Mind you, under the best of circumstances, getting to your feet with snowshoes on is no easy task. I don't remember how long we sat in the snow laughing before someone from the hotel came and untangled us, helping us to our feet. We ended up at a gorgeous lodge for a wonderful lunch before we were delivered back to our hotel—in a horse-drawn sleigh!

When our week in St. Moritz came to an end, Elizabeth took a train to see her family in Austria, and I headed off to see a bit more of Switzerland. My plan was to stay in a lovely hotel at each destination and dine at the hotel so that I would feel safe. The next day, I planned to look around the hotel, get my bearings, eat dinner, and go to bed early. The following day I would hire a guide to show me about the city, and I would then spend the last day exploring and discovering the city on my own before boarding the train to visit another city. I did just that. I stayed at the Baur au Lac in Zurich and the Beau-Rivage in Geneva.

After a beautiful Sunday morning hike in the snow I arrived back at my hotel with the intent of going to my room for a rest. I heard music and gaiety down the hall and went to the desk to inquire about the celebration. The concierge told me that every Sunday they had what they called Tea Dancing. Live music along with tea and tea sandwiches was quite a favorite among the hotel guests and guests from neighboring hotels. On the way to my room, I said to myself, *What is the worst thing that could happen? Nobody asks me to dance, and I enjoy a live band and have a little tea and sandwiches.* It didn't take me long to shower, change, and find the Tea Dance. I was seated at a nice table where I could watch the dancers and hear the band. I ordered my tea and sandwiches, and to my great surprise, a young man came up to me and asked me to dance.

We danced and then he returned me to my table, where the men practically lined up for a dance with me. I was having so much fun as I danced with each one. Finally a handsome German man asked me to dance and instead of returning me to the table and leaving, he sat down and we ate dinner together. We then took a wonderful stroll in the evening snow, and he didn't speak a word of English. So we smiled a lot!

Each evening at dinner I would sit down alone at a table, and I was astonished because I never ended up dining alone. Guests would come by my table and ask me to join them. I met such interesting people from all parts of Europe. It was a magical time. I accomplished more than just a change of venue and a change of scene on this trip. I now began to have confidence in myself, seeing that people, knowing nothing about my background, wanted to meet me. I was not someone's wife or someone's mother; I was just me. I came home a much more confident woman, with the ability to now make choices and decisions about my life.

Elizabeth and I stayed in touch with Christmas cards and occasional notes, and she came to stay with me at Amber Hills on a visit to California. But it wasn't until I set about to write this book that we got together to reminisce about our time in St. Moritz. We were destined to be there the exact same week, and though we were both fine with the fact that we were traveling alone, we ended up having a wonderful time together. It was therapeutic not only to laugh so much, but to be with someone who knew very little of my past. Fun, skiing, laughing, and dancing took center stage, and we were playmates, living for the moment with no regard for the past or the future. Elizabeth was surprised to finally learn how impactful this trip was for my recovery and sense of self. But what didn't surprise either of us was that a lifelong friendship was born that week.

## Elizabeth Juen Waltz: Friend and Ski Enthusiast

It all started with a scarf.

As a reward for myself from myself, for the hard work I had put in at my real-estate firm, I decided on my first ever trip alone—to St. Moritz for a ski holiday. I chose the Palace Hotel because I wanted sheer luxury and sophistication. I had never stayed at such an exquisitely appointed hotel, and it was the first time I ever saw a man wearing a full-length fur coat. I recognized him as the German playboy Gunter Sachs who was married to Brigitte Bardot in the late sixties. But this was the ambiance of the Palace Hotel, and it was fascinating.

I was a certified ski instructor but did not plan on revealing that information as I wanted to learn new techniques and ways of teaching. Attending the reception in the hotel the first evening, I was impressed to see how well-dressed and elegant the guests were, but it was all a little too subdued for me. Just as I was about to return to my room, I spotted a beautiful woman across the room with a scarf tied around her red hair in the most fashionable way. I had spent many years of my life working in Buckingham Palace, and I had also worked for a brief time for King Leopold. Having worked with many people who have presence, I knew presence, and this woman had it. I was quite taken with her persona and thought to myself, *I bet she is fun*, so I made my way over to say hello with the hope of at least finding out how she tied that scarf so elegantly. After a few introductory words we both agreed that although it was lovely, the reception was just a little too tame for our tastes. We trotted through the snow to a little chalet where we enjoyed a lovely dinner and fun conversation. Though we were at different levels of skiing, we were both planning on having an instructor guide us around the mountain the next day. Skiing was delightful, and when my instructor realized how well I could ski, he asked me how many days I had signed on for. When I told him four days, he winked and said, "We are going to have a good time." Even though the snow wasn't as deep as it could have been, we had a fabulous time together.

After my first day of an amazing time, I left a note for my new pal to see if she would like to meet up again for dinner and checked with the desk for the correct spelling of her name: Glorya with a *y*. That was the beginning of what we both remember to be a most carefree time, filled with dinners, dancing, and incredible amounts of laughter. We connected like children and had the kind of fun playmates have, enjoying the incredible fun of the present with no regard for the past or the future. I did not know a great deal about Glorya's past, and she did not know a great deal about me. Years later she shared with me how therapeutic and healing our time was for her. I didn't remind her of anything from her past and had no reason at all to feel sorry for her, which is what she set out to escape. What we both knew was that we were on a ski holiday to have fun, and we did just that. Each evening after a full day of skiing, we would go out for dinner and dancing either at our hotel or somewhere nearby. It was all very civilized and elegant: The men would come to our table, bow, ask one of us to dance, and then escort us back to the table, kiss our hands, and thank us for the dance. It was very sophisticated and very European. I don't believe any bowing and hand-kissing goes on in the nightclubs of America—at least not of the type we were enjoying.

I will never forget the vision, forever imprinted in my mind, of Glorya the day she left the Palace Hotel. St. Moritz is a very small town with a very small train station, and it definitely had the only Rolls Royce around. There was Glorya, with her flaming red hair tied so incredibly with the scarf adorning her head, with all of her bags in the back of the Rolls. It was all very Great Gatsby, and as she pulled away, I felt as if I were in the last scene of a movie. It would not, however, be the last scene of our friendship, which would endure for many years to come. Glorya is as beautiful inside as she is outside, and her presence has only become even more brilliant as she has moved so gracefully through life.

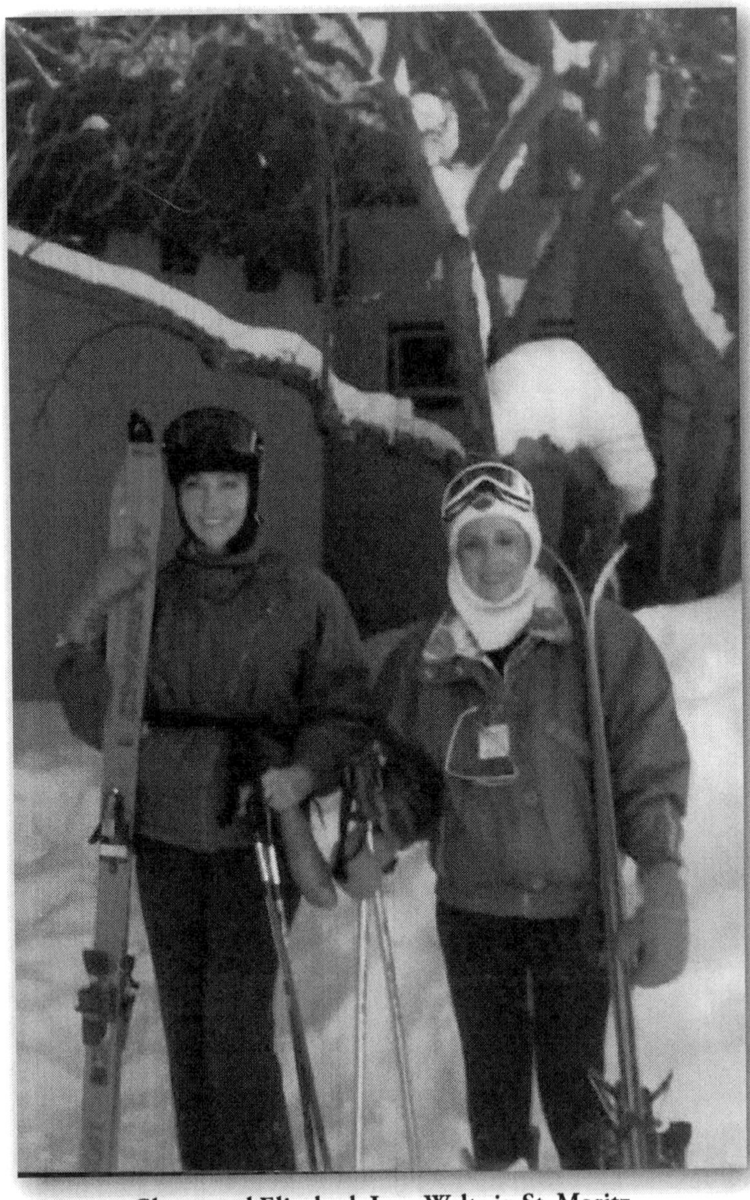

**Glorya and Elizabeth Juen Waltz in St. Moritz**

# Just a Fashion Statement

I am a fashion person, and fashion is not only about clothes, it's about all kinds of change.

—Karl Lagerfeld

Since change was what my life had been all about, fashion fell right into the mix. I grew up loving fashion and making a great deal of my own wardrobe, just to be different, just to have a change. I dress to entertain myself and to express my happiness. I love new styles, but that's not always what it's about. It's about knowing yourself and expressing who you are. I've never been afraid to put together a different look, and I am usually complimented on my style. I have many favorite designers, but I also know something special when I see it, regardless of name or price.

I love Paris so much that I bought an apartment and enjoyed it for many years. In springtime, wintertime, whatever time, I just love the city, the art, the walking, the museums, and, of course, the fashion. Over the years I learned the city very well, and I would take different routes, walking for hours, people-watching and window-shopping. In my travels I came across a little dress shop called Anne Lowe, two doors away from the famous and fabulous hotel Le Bristol Paris on Rue Saint-Honoré. This darling little shop was filled with clothing from well-known designers and many unknown designers. It didn't take long for me to get to know the owner, Suzy Goei, a lovely woman with long dark hair and a captivating smile. I liked her immediately. She never pushed to sell but was always helpful when needed. I had a lot of fun finding interesting belts, sweaters, and skirts, and had a great time putting together fun outfits.

On one of my visits, Suzy told me she had been in business for thirty years and had never seen ensembles put together the way I put them together. She loved my offbeat choices and wanted to know if I would be interested in going with her to wholesale factories to pick out new inventory for the store. Wow! I was very flattered and told her I would love such an adventure. A few days later we were off together to her favorite manufacturers. She tried on clothes, I took photos, and together we made choices that we thought would do well at the shop. After a lovely lunch together, the deal was sealed, and there was never a time I visited Paris that I did not find myself visiting Suzy. Of course, I never left her shop empty-handed. She became one of my dearest friends. Since giving up my apartment in Paris, I now stay with Suzy at her apartment, and when she is in Los Angeles, she stays with me. How can I not love fashion even more? On top of everything else, it brought me a forever friend.

## Bobbi Homari: Personal Assistant and Friend

I had the pleasure of meeting Glorya through a mutual friend and a shared love of dance. As a native Hungarian, I came to this country when I realized it was the only way I was going to survive. I was soon hired by Glorya to be her personal assistant. In reality, I feel that Glorya was the one assisting me with everything in my life, beginning with style. When I first met Glorya, all I wore was black: black skirts, black pants…black. It wasn't appropriate to wear color in my country, and I remember my mother only wearing black. I started checking out everything about Glorya, and she even helped me with my English. Instead of going to a job, it was like coming home. She was my teacher and my mentor. She gave me advice on everything from wardrobe to reading literature, with grace and love.

I loved everything about how she dressed and how she designed her beautiful home. She put everything together like an artist—which she is. I actually take great pride in the fact that I like to copy as much of what Glorya does as possible. I know that imitation is the highest form of flattery, and I have no shame when it comes to my mentor. If there was something Glorya did that I liked, I found a way to copy it as best I could. I loved the way she hung her little antique purses on hooks along the wall and had great fun doing the same in my room at my home. Of course, it didn't end there.

During the years I worked for Glorya as her assistant I learned a great deal. Unfortunately, it was during the years that the scoundrel J. Ron Reed was in her life. He knew I was fiercely protective of her and tried his best to get rid of me. When he would tell me that Glorya was unhappy with my work, I would reply that if she was unhappy, I was sure she would let me know. He didn't scare me, but I knew he was the worst possible news.

One of the things I admired so much about Glorya was her discipline when it came to her exercise regime. She never missed a morning in her gym! I would peek in every morning when I arrived for work, and there she would be, without fail. The reason she looked so magnificent in anything she wore was because she had the figure to back it up, a figure she worked as hard to keep as anything else she put effort into.

Glorya modeled for me how to be generous, smart, full of good taste, and above all else, how to be loyal. Loyalty means more to Glorya than anything else. And she will be loyal to a fault. You really have to screw up badly many times before Glorya gives you the heave-ho. Above all else, Glorya never made me feel that she was more than me, or had more than me, and that is so very rare.

She is so giving that it makes it very difficult for me to understand her children's treatment of her. Laura is a sweetheart, but the other three are icebergs. I don't understand it, but I've witnessed it. I remember an event she invited her children to, and no one showed up. I sat next to her and felt lucky and blessed. Her children are the ones I feel sad for because of what they are missing. I doubt that they will ever wake up and realize it. How sad.

I am so proud to have Glorya in my life, not just because of what she has done for me but also because of what she has done, and still does, to better the lives of others. One of her gifts went for scholarships for single mothers at the W. American Jewish University. Glorya told me once that if the mother works hard to support the family, then her children will grow up with a wholesome work ethic. As a hardworking mother this touched me and spoke to my heart. In 2012, Glorya was given the Presidential Award by the National Dance Education Organization for her shared vision that dance is an "art form whose benefits to mankind goes far beyond entertainment." What a fabulous accomplishment for this wonderful woman who cannot only help humankind but can also help and has helped one eternally grateful woman from Hungary.

## Joseph Dyrcz: Hairdresser and Friend

I grew up in Wisconsin, truly dreaming of designing gorgeous high-style hair for people who make a great difference in the world. I personally created, owned, and managed three salons with great success. After fourteen years, taking a leap of faith, I decided to begin a new life in Los Angeles.

A slim, well-dressed, and striking woman walked into Klaus Coiffure Hair Salon in Brentwood looking for a new, exciting hair design from a new hairdresser! It was nothing more than fate and the roll of the dice that it turned out to be me. It was 1984, a year after Glorya lost her husband, and she was making a lot of changes, her look being one of them. My first impression was that she had a beautiful face and unique style of dressing.

Glorya and I hit it off immediately. For thirty-two years, I have had the great pleasure of playing with Glorya's unending shades of red, wavy, sumptuous hair. I have given her more high styles in hair than any other client in my entire forty-five years. Glorya loves to laugh, and she just lights up when that giggle slips out. She is full of hope and wonderment. Considering her position and her affluence, Glorya is the most down-to-earth person I could ever hope to meet. Having her as one of my very special clients has shown me that my gift of accessing the soul of my clients by bringing out the very best in them rewards me as much as them.

Glorya's class and style are immediately evident. What is not so evident until you get to know her is her gift for being warm and nurturing. On innumerable occasions, she has invited me to Amber Hills, or Chateau de Liberté (her new home) in Beverly Hills, to create a new look for her event of that day or evening. When I'm helping Glorya look even more chic, it seems we invariably end up in her closet, picking out everything from shoes to belts and accessories to complement her hairstyle. (Her closets are ones that a gay man would never come out of.) She treats me with love and respect and trust and truly makes me feel like part of her family. Her ability to make people feel good just comes so naturally, and we have on many occasions discussed our similar Midwest roots. Over the years I had the opportunity to work with her three daughters; however, the gal that made a lasting impression is her granddaughter April. When I was first introduced to her, I saw a Greek goddess. Her eyes and dimples were clearly from her beautiful mother, Laura. She has grown into a beautiful woman with children, but for me she will always be the six-year-old sweetheart with dimples.

Glorya is a truly unique, special, intensely giving soul who is intertwined in my life, as I am in hers. She is a rare human being. I am incredibly blessed to be able to share my life journey with her.

As I reflect back on our thirty-two years together, I realize that paths are meant to cross. I am fortunate to have Glorya woven into the tapestry of my life. She is the essence of giving, has inspired me to give back, and brings joy to my life.

## Sue Lapin: Friend

I write this for a special friend and a "sister that I chose." We have been friends since Glorya's daughter Gayl and my oldest son, Jeff, were in the same class in grammar school. There has never been a cross word between us. Glorya has been a true friend—loyal, sensitive, wonderful, and mature, ready to give advice or have fun, always available and trustworthy in sharing all secrets. I know that they are safe.

You are my sunshine, dear Glorya. Thank you for being you. I love you forever.

## Tae-Hee Danos: Painter and Friend

Life is a long journey. It is wonderful to be able to find extraordinary people as companions.

I met Glorya on one of those beautiful, sunny California days on her property, Amber Hills, on Mandeville Canyon Road. I was a guest at the house of a mutual friend, Das Silverman. Das and Glorya shared two interests: Chinese cuisine and dance. Das was a very accomplished Argentinian tango and swing dancer. Glorya and Das travelled together to Buenos Aires, Paris, and Lyon on a mission to promote a dance theater in Los Angeles.

Das was one of my closest friends, a second mother to me. She knew how keen I was on garden design and asked if I would like to visit Glorya's amazing garden. I was literally mesmerized by it. It was more of a park on the canyon, with trees, all kinds of flowers, a waterfall, and exotic birds. Glorya stepped out of the house, and we met. I can still taste the watermelon smoothie she offered, saying it came from her vegetable garden. I learned that she had just purchased an apartment in Paris. We promised each other to meet when she came over to France. After she had finalized the acquisition of her pied–à–terre on Avenue Montaigne, we spent hours browsing around the flea market, searching for rare pieces. Glorya had decided to decorate her flat without the help of a decorator. It was great fun. She has a great eye for treasures, has her own taste, and loves to mix and match. It was on our first Parisian lunch together that I discovered that she was totally simple in her taste for food. She picked a moules-frites restaurant at the flea market and loved it!

We went together to exhibits, shows, and four-star restaurants, always having fun and a lively time of it. As we got to know each other, we shared stories from our past. I learned about her life and discovered that what we had in common was our love of life and our gift for surviving. We had both survived tragedies, loss, and grief. We both had had to struggle and had never given up.

I was fascinated when I heard that she wished to support dance as well as cancer research and children's health care. Among her many commitments, helping needy children get proper eye treatment was one of her goals.

I had my own problem with my left eye. My eyes did not align properly, and this made me self-conscious. Glorya introduced me to a specialist who performed a surgery that could correct my problem. In 2009 I made an appointment as she suggested with Dr. Joseph Demer at the Jules Stein Institute at UCLA. It was a burden to have to undergo surgery in a foreign country, but Glorya insisted that if anyone could correct the problem, it was Dr. Demer. I had had three previous surgeries that were not successful, but I would go through the procedure one more time if he could help me.

I vividly recall hearing Glorya's soft voice as I was waking up. She was there for me. I felt so relieved; all my problems had vanished, I gained self-confidence, and I no longer hesitated to talk to strangers. I even started learning Argentinian tango. I decided to take dancing lessons in 2013, when my husband recovered from cancer.

After I returned home to Paris that year, I put my heart and soul into learning how to dance the tango. I now have become comfortable with my looks and feel good about myself. I have earnestly taken tango classes and workshops, and now am adept at dancing the tango, which has allowed me to join in marathons and festivals all over the world.

I also joined an association that promotes Argentinian tango and culture. We are spreading the word in my hometown. With my newfound self-confidence, I'm feeling happy. Dancing has a great effect on body and mind. One walks better and feels more balanced.

As you see, Glorya has done wonders for me. I think children should be taught to dance in kindergarten. Moving gracefully can help socially and professionally. Energy is a great drive.

Glorya and I share a passion, but we also share the little things that happen in everyday life. We talk freely to each other and help each other to grow.

I can only hope that, one day, she will also find the time to dance. It's her turn to be on the dance floor.

Thank you, Glorya! Dance must go on!

Author's note: Tae is a special friend of mine, and I cherish her. She is a native of South Korea. Her love for travel, meeting people, and discovering other cultures brought her to France. She left Korea without knowing a word of French, learned the language, and became a hotel manager. Phillipe, her husband, had cancer and at this writing is in remission. Tae read everything she could get her hands on to help him survive, especially concentrating on his diet.

She is a gardener and a lovely watercolor painter. Tae sticks with whatever she tackles until she has perfected it. She is one in a million.

# Enver White: Guardian Angel Extraordinaire

THIS CHAPTER IS VERY LONG and intentionally so. I've written it to honor someone who stood by me in the hardest twenty years of my life.

The first year after Don's death was a blur of loss, emotional pain, and great fear regarding what was to come next. There was not much I knew with certainty except that I wanted to create a beautiful and tranquil space for myself at the ranch. I knew the project was a huge one and would occupy my mind. I at least was cognizant enough to know I needed that. What I did not know was that I was about to meet a very special person who would help me create something I desperately needed in my life: magic.

Enver White came to me through an agency. I had finally gotten to a point where I was ready to have someone live on the property and take care of—but more important, transform—the grounds. We sat together in my living room as he told me what he had been doing since he arrived in this country a few years earlier from Sri Lanka. He worked as a handyman, carpenter, and painter, and he loved gardening and caring for any and all animals. It was all rather ordinary, and I didn't find any of it very impressive. It wasn't until he started telling me about Sri Lanka and his life there that I sat on the edge of the couch. He was of Irish and Danish ancestry but was born circa 1930 in Sri Lanka, which was under British rule at the time.

Forty-four miles of water separate India from Sri Lanka; however, because of the lush greenery, the Indian elephants migrated there when Adams Bridge, a chain of shoals, connected Sri Lanka to India. In 1480, a cyclone wiped out the bridge, and Sri Lanka became a separate island, holding the elephants hostage, so to speak.

The zoo in Sri Lanka was world renowned and the only zoo with sixteen trained elephants. It was Enver's job to take care of the elephants, and he did so for thirty-three years, never losing an elephant. He also tended the zoo's exquisite botanical gardens and was well-versed in botany. I sat spellbound while he told me stories of taking care of the animals at the zoo, explaining that they were his family and he loved them as such. Of course, his references from the zoo were amazing. In 1971, his wife fell ill, but they couldn't get her to the hospital in time. Roads were blocked due to an insurgency, and she died. Eventually he left his son and daughter with family and ventured to America on a six-month visa. His wife's family was already here, and he managed to get a green card during the amnesty of the Reagan administration. He only returned to Sri Lanka once, however.

For many reasons, it made Enver sad to think of going back. One of the biggest reasons was that when the zoo was under Enver's wing, it was heralded as the most beautiful zoo in the world. It broke his heart to eventually hear that now when tourists visit the zoo, the smell is so bad that they are forced to hold their noses. I explained to Enver that I was reluctant to have a man on the property, as I had had some previous bad experiences. I was living there alone and was really quite uncomfortable. I did not realize that in Enver I had found not only a phenomenal landscape artist but, more important, my guardian angel. We decided to give it a whirl. He and his companion moved into the guesthouse across from the main house, and I told him that after six months, if all was going well, I would give him a raise. Under my tutelage, the transformation took place.

Enver's first mission at Amber Hills was to clear the heavy junglelike growth that started at the gate off the canyon road and continued for a good half mile along both sides of the long driveway to the house. This alone took him and the crew five months. In the early seventies Don had planted Canary Island pine trees throughout the property, and they had grown quite tall, messy, and very combustible. These were removed, leaving valuable, protected oak trees that were very beautiful. Enver had uncovered deer bones in the clearing of the upper mountain. This, in tandem with some other clues, had us suspecting that we also had at least one mountain lion roaming around. Mountain lion visits happened, but they were infrequent.

In addition to everyday rodent problems that needed to be addressed, the deer were a huge problem, as they would eat all the vegetation on the property. It used to frighten me when I would see a lot of them. It would not be unusual to see up to sixteen at a time. And they were not afraid. I guess they instinctually knew the ranch was a safe haven, and that I would not harm them. They had pretty much moved in and were multiplying rapidly. One day, as Enver and I were walking by the main house, we saw a group of deer eating our lovely flowers on the hillside. Enver got his rifle and fired a shot into the air. The deer scattered, but by the time I made it back to the main house I got a call from the gate. It was the police. I told them I had not called them, but they said a neighbor had reported hearing a gunshot, and they were there to check it out. At this point in time, I did not have a closed circuit monitor, and I was reluctant to let callers through the gate even when they professed to be the police. Anyone could say they were the police. I told them all was well, but that obviously did not satisfy them because before long a helicopter was buzzing overhead. I reluctantly opened the gate. Not realizing my driveway was a half mile long, the police left their cars at the gate and walked up the driveway. Once there is an entry through the gate, the road lights go on, but they only stay on for five minutes. Not knowing the police were on foot, I did not warn them that the lights would only stay on for five minutes. After what seemed to be twenty minutes, six huge policemen arrived at the front door. I greeted them with Enver and my six-month-old Rhodesian ridgeback puppy, Troy. I had told Enver not to mention that he fired the rifle into the air.

Enver and I tried to keep our faces straight when one of the policemen told us that when the lights went off, they had all "hit the deck" for at least ten minutes, waiting for the other shoe to drop. After they checked the house out, convinced that all was in order and nothing sinister had occured, I explained to them my hesitancy about letting someone claiming to be the police in through the gate. One of the burly officers told me that in the future I should ask for their badge number and call the police station to verify that they are indeed bona fide policemen. His advice was a day late and a dollar short, but it was still a good lesson learned. Since they never did ask us if we had fired a shot we weren't about to volunteer it. I figured it was a case of no harm, no foul. After they left, along with the helicopter, Enver and I collapsed into laughter at the imaginary bullet we had both dodged, and this moment of duplicity and the secret we now shared was a true bonding experience for both of us. The next day I hired a company to fence off the entire perimeter of the ranch to keep the deer out. It worked.

Little by little, the ranch property transformation spearheaded by Enver took off. If Enver could visualize something, he could do it. And his visionary powers were acute. I called him the King of Recycle. He never wasted anything and was a wiz at transplanting flowers instead of buying new ones. He transplanted over a thousand ice plant snippings to other areas of the grounds, and white and purple daisies were transplanted as well as calla lilies by the dozens. The calla lilies grew to be so large that Enver said they were the largest he had ever seen. We brought in fruit trees, beautiful daffodil and iris bulbs, and hundreds of rosebushes. He turned the old riding arena into a vegetable garden, and we would soon be harvesting vegetables. My goal was to have many things blooming at different times of the year so that the property would always be ablaze in beauty and color. Next to the lake, I placed beautiful and bright-colored totem poles that I purchased from an artist named Horton in Inglewood, California. Enver would repair them and repaint them, as well as my beautiful wooden carousel horse, every four or five years to keep them from looking weather-beaten from sun and rain. I loved those totems and enjoyed the happiness I felt when I looked at them.

When I moved from Amber Hills, I donated five totem poles to a nursery school. I left the rest behind and can only hope that they are still bringing joy. I had other sculptures and art pieces placed about the property, and they all had one special thing in common, which was the reason I would acquire them to begin with. They were almost all whimsical and brought me joy when I looked at them. I designed a beautiful door for the entrance to my bedroom suite that was two tango dancers etched in glass. It was framed in a huge metal casing that ended up being so heavy that it was impossible to open and close the door. After the carpenters removed the door and reworked it in wood, I was left with this huge metal door frame that was really quite magnificent. I had Enver and the crew prop it on an angle on the trail that led to the gazebo. We made a sculpture out of it. For me, it signified a doorway to the next adventure. We don't know where this new adventure will take us until we are brave enough to step through the door. This is a reminder for me that something may not fit right away, but that doesn't mean it could not become something else entirely.

I found many of my art pieces while traveling. Several of my sculptures came from Israel. On one of my visits with my daughter Gayl who was living in Israel with her family, I discovered a sculptress by the name of Naomi Schindler. She sculpted people in a contemporary motif that drew me in immediately. I bought several pieces and had them shipped to Amber Hills. Since they were on the contemporary side, along with my whimsical and imaginative pieces, my artwork became very eclectic. But once again, it was meaningful to me and gave me a great sense of joy.

When I would visit my Paris apartment on Avenue Montaigne across from the Plaza Athénée, there was almost nothing I found more fascinating than walking around admiring the art and sculpture. Two of my favorite pieces of sculpture, outdoor statues made of resin by an artist who signs her work as "Josepha a Paris," came from one of my many trips. One was placed across from the front door. I could also enjoy it from my upstairs office window. The other one was placed in a turnout area coming up the driveway. The brightly colored buxom girls, as I call them, are just pure whimsy and fun, and they now have special spots at my Beverly Hills home, Chateau de Liberté.

I could never have devoted time to this project when Don was alive and all four children were home. Now the ranch was my spouse and my children, and it was getting my undivided attention. In time, the white wooden fences around the lake weathered and were replaced with concrete fences so that they would not chip and peel. Enver watched as the first section was completed by a crew that I hired, and then he himself finished the rest of the fencing. Several different colors of bougainvillea were trained to grow along the fences, adding beautiful color. We added water lilies and lotus flowers to the lake, and some of our goldfish grew so huge they looked like koi. Four-inch catfish grew to be four feet! Of course, not only had Enver and his crew accomplished all of this work, it also had to be maintained.

One of the most important areas of maintenance was fire clearance. Every year all brush needed to be cleared within three hundred yards of the house. Every time this clearance took place, Enver would capture between ten and fifteen rattle snakes. He would gather them in a pail and call me over to hear them hiss. Eventually he would give me the rattles. Enver's knowledge of animals, including snakes, from his thirty-three years of experience at the zoo was about to prove not only invaluable but, in fact, lifesaving. My mother was living with me at the ranch after my father died, along with Enver's companion, Rita, who looked after her. Rita would spend hours sitting in the yard reading to my mother. One afternoon a rattlesnake bit Rita's hand while she was reading to my mom. We were in a hurry to get her to the hospital until Enver intervened. He knew that being able to take the snake along with us could prove to save her life. He also knew that when a rattlesnake bites, it too is affected. The snake becomes lethargic and can be found within a ten-foot radius of where the attack took place. Enver found the snake curled up, and he captured it to take along with us to UCLA. Rita's hand was horrifically swollen, but having the snake proved to be crucial to the antivenin they administered. She was very uncomfortable for a few weeks.

One of the most beautiful qualities about Enver was that he never questioned me. Actually, this had its good and bad sides. One day as I drove down the driveway headed to a luncheon, I saw a tree that looked like it should be removed. Motioning Enver to the car, I pointed out the tree and told him to remove it. By the time I got to the restaurant for lunch, I had changed my mind about having the tree removed and put a call in to Enver to tell him so. Too late! Speedy Gonzalez, as I called him, had already removed the tree.

Enver was fiercely loyal to me, and quite protective. If he knew I was out for the evening, he would stay up until he heard my car go over the bridge. He had strict instructions that absolutely no one was to be let through the gate when I was out of town, and he never made exceptions. He would even turn my children away. As Enver put it, "If Mrs. Kaufman told me to burn the house down, I would burn the house down. If Mrs. Kaufman asks me, 'Enver, is it a good idea to burn the house down?' then I will tell her, 'No, this is not a good idea.'" Quite simply, I don't think I would have been able to remain on the property without Enver. He was a proud man and knew I trusted him literally with my life. There were many times when I would demonstrate my loyalty to him, and he would beam with pride. When I was converting the game room adjacent to the tennis court into a dance studio, Enver had a disagreement about the work with the contractor I had hired to spearhead the transformation. When the contractor confronted me about Enver, I told him in no uncertain terms, "You are here today and gone tomorrow; Enver is here forever." This tickled Enver so. The look on his face was just one of a very appreciative man. I saw that look on his face one other time, when the bridge over the lake needed to be reinforced. The engineer I had brought up to estimate what needed to be done was quite adamant that an expert carpenter would be needed to do the work. When I made it clear that it wouldn't be a problem and that I had an expert carpenter working for me, I turned to shoot a smile to an already beaming Enver. In Enver's book there was just no substitute for loyalty and being appreciated. And we read from the same book. For me, loyalty is number one. It is everything.

One thing that weighed heavily on Enver was the fact that he missed his children terribly but was having great difficulty getting them to America. I wrote letters to Congress to help bring his children here, and eventually they made it to California. His son Kevin moved into the guesthouse with his father and worked on the property for many years as well. Kevin, who was so much like his father, loved to put a smile on my face. Once when I went on an extended trip to Europe, Kevin moved all the furniture on the first floor of the house, stripped the floors, and polished them. When I arrived back home, I guess my face lit up with delight, because so did Kevin's! I really don't know which of us was happier, but I walked around in my socks for days to protect the beautiful floors. Like his father, Kevin also loved the gardens and the grounds and worked hard to keep them lush and beautiful. Kevin was a genius at bringing a little of the grounds into my home. He would make the most exquisite flower arrangements and place them all over the house. Each arrangement was a work of art made using cuttings from the garden that I never would have thought to use myself. I began to plan brunches so that I could entertain my guests during the daytime and they could enjoy strolling the beautiful, serene, parklike grounds that we had created. On Sunday mornings, I would take the dogs and walk up past the waterfall and take the trail to the gazebo that overlooked the property. Comfy lounge chairs awaited any visitor who knew about the gazebo's existence. I would sit with my coffee, dogs, and newspaper and literally do nothing but read and enjoy my lovely surroundings. It helped keep me focused and appreciative of the smallest things in life, like enjoying peace and quiet and the beauty of nature. When the sun began to set each evening, it would cast an amber glow on the hills surrounding the ranch. It was these beautiful and peaceful moments every day that I found not only comforting but inspirational as well. It seemed to me that anything that goes through such a transformation and brings such beauty and joy is deserving of a new name. Along with the rebirth of the ranch came that new name—Amber Hills. It was indeed magical, just as I had envisioned, and Enver and the crew had made it a reality.

Probably more than just about anything, Enver loved animals. Every spring, we would have a new crop of baby ducklings, and they would become Enver's pets. However, since it was hard to keep them away from the hawks, it was a heartbreaking situation. In his quest to find something a little more lasting, Enver got himself a little pet cockatiel named Tippy. He got to enjoy part of the day outdoors in his cage in front of Enver's house. Tippy talked quite a bit, and he and Enver would have little conversations. It was a very sad day when the child of a friend who had come to visit me simply opened the door to the cage and little Tippy flew away. I felt horrible, and Enver was just devastated. To make up for the loss, he built an aviary behind his house, and he soon had it filled with cockatiels, finches, lovebirds, and parakeets. The collection grew to include about two hundred birds, and they chirped and warbled very beautiful melodies. Soon we built several aviaries under the oaks surrounding the lake, and they housed parrots and macaws. The two macaws were exquisite. One was red and the other shades of blue. Between the birds and the dogs, Enver was in heaven. And I must say that even with two hundred birds, there was never a dirty aviary or any kind of odor. Just as he had done at the Sri Lanka zoo, Enver kept the animals and their compounds pristine.

Although he had his miniature zoo, Enver would often tell me that he missed the zoo and its animals in Sri Lanka. There were no problems there, and the other workers were his friends. He didn't think he could ever be as happy as he was when he was working at the zoo. I had two female Rhodesian ridgebacks, Blaze and Amber, who had bred with a champion ridgeback, Rocky. When Blaze and Amber were close to giving birth, Enver hooked up a monitor in his house to listen for the signs that the pups were coming. When the time came and they began to whimper, Enver delivered the puppies in the guest room of the main house, which we had already prepared for whelping. Between the two females, we had sixteen pups! All of them were named after a color—Rusty, Copper, Taffy, Sienna, Coffee, Mocha, Silver, Cinnamon, Mango, Violet, Scarlet, Indigo, and Denim. I know I'm forgetting a few. After all these years I can't remember all the names, but what I do remember is how much time, love, and work Enver put into raising and caring for the pups. He never lost one of the litter, which is amazing. Each of the dogs was well trained and always clean. Their kennel, of course, was always spotless. He had put so much work and love into training them that I told him he could keep whatever money he made when he sold them. I gave two away, Enver ended up selling five of them, and we kept seven. One cool crisp morning, Enver and I took one of our walks down to the gate with the dogs. On this gorgeous California day, they romped along beside us down to the gate and back. On the way back up the hill, I did all the talking because Enver was gasping for air and unable to speak! I was used to working out in the gym daily and never missed my session on the treadmill. When we got back to the house and Enver could breathe again, he told me that he was wrong about something. He had found another job and another home that he loved as much as the zoo in Sri Lanka. And that home was here with me. He told me I had always treated him kindly, fairly, and with respect. He added that he never had to ask for anything because I always offered it to him first, whether it be a raise, a vacation, or permission to get more birds. I felt a rise of emotion as my breath caught in my throat, and now it was my turn to be unable to speak. For Enver and me, it always worked both ways. We were there for each other, each looking out for the other.

When Enver retired at seventy-five years old, I bought him his own home in Norwalk, where he still lives today. I only asked one thing of Enver in return: that whenever I traveled, he would pick me up at the airport when I came home. He was thrilled at our bargain, and it gave us a chance to catch up whenever he drove me. At this writing, when I arrive at the airport from a trip, at eighty-four years old, Enver picks me up and escorts me to be sure I have arrived safely.

# The Magic of India

OF ALL THE WONDERFUL AND exciting places in the world, I had always wanted to see India, a land of mystery and fascinating culture. It was 1986. Don had been gone just a little over three years, and it was time for me to have an adventure of this magnitude on my own. A great opportunity presented itself to me when I was introduced to a woman who owned a travel agency. She was putting together a tour of India, and only three doctors and their wives had committed to the trip. They were very receptive to me joining their trip even though I would be a single. I was extremely excited, in anticipation of a great adventure.

As fate would have it, I had a friend who had attended the University of Southern California with an Indian man, Lalite Thaper, who came from an illustrious family; his father was even a maharajah (a great ruler of his day). My friend offered to write to Lalite, enclosing a copy of my travel itinerary. After examining my travel plans, Lalite wrote back, "Glorya will need a vacation after her vacation as there are too many things on the itinerary for her to enjoy them all without getting overly exhausted." He also sent all his contact information along with an invitation for me to join him for dinner the night of my arrival in New Delhi. My flight didn't arrive until 4:00 a.m. India time, and our dinner rendezvous was at 8:00 p.m. that evening.

The city was bustling. Coincidentally it was November 1, Diwali, the festival of lights, an ancient Hindu festival where everyone in India, rich or poor, fat or skinny, gets dressed up to participate in a special five-day celebration that includes good food, games, and fireworks. First I went to a lovely home with friends from California where we viewed an exquisite display of fireworks. Lalite sent a car to pick me up and bring me to his estate. I was greeted at the door by a servant and ushered into a beautiful room where Lalite was sitting on a throne-like chair. He was wearing a turban on his head, and a red dot was painted on the center of his forehead. It was all very intriguing and just as I had imagined. He introduced himself, and I thanked him for his kind invitation for dinner. We became acquainted, and I found him extremely friendly and intelligent. I knew he was educated, but the way he was sitting on the throne was a little intimidating and I wasn't prepared for his friendliness. Yet I was certainly taken with him. Lalite smoked a lot of cigarettes, and I would see a servant tend to him every time he put one out in the ashtray. I later noticed that Lalite had a buzzer located on the armrest of his throne. He would press it, and his servant would empty the ashtray automatically then leave the room.

Soon the doorbell rang, and a friend of his entered the house. I was introduced, and we all visited. Before long, the bell rang again, and another of his friends joined us. One of the gentlemen was the owner of a company that was on a par with the DuPont Company, and the other fellow owned the largest oriental-rug company in India. It did not take me long to realize that this was where the men gathered to play cards, as that was part of their tradition. I was, of course, invited to dinner, but when I saw the handwriting on the wall, I told Lalite that I was extremely tired and would like to go back to the hotel. He was startled and gave me an interesting look. I found out later that no one ever would have left as I did, for fear of insulting him. But it turned out that Lalite liked my spirit. Yes, I was getting better at speaking up for myself, and a man actually admired the quality. He invited me to dinner for the following evening and said he would be taking me to the finest Indian restaurant.

The next evening, I was picked up again. Much to my surprise Lalite's house was full of his friends; he had invited them especially to meet me. I met some lovely people, and the women were all decked out in the most beautiful jewelry. We were served dinner on elegant sterling-silver plates that had been made especially for Indian food and handed down from generation to generation. The plates had little compartments for the individual portions, creating a feast for the eyes. Though some of the food was quite exotic, I truly enjoyed everything that was served. What amazed me the most was the dessert—chocolate candy dipped in real silver. I was told that in the old days this chocolate delicacy was dipped in real gold. Forget the expense and the beauty of the dessert, I just wondered how healthy it would be to eat. It was a delightful evening. Lalite introduced me to many illustrious and entertaining friends, and I was starting to understand and enjoy the traditions of the privileged in this amazing country.

The next day, I joined my group of doctors and their wives for a tour of the city. Our guide fascinated all of us with his knowledge of history and flair for telling a story. He captivated us with details of such historic events as the British Empire's expansion to include India. Of course this meant that the British dominated world trade and in effect controlled the economy of India. As I walked along the streets of New Delhi I saw many beggars and a lot of poverty. I also saw a country that was full of wonderful colors. The streets and shops were ablaze with brilliant colors of clothing, tapestry, and rugs. I loved being there and hearing the history of the country. I did not see anyone wearing black or white, which was so different from the United States.

Lalite introduced me to his sister, Raj, and we hit it off right away. She took me to a seamstress who made lovely colorful cotton outfits. The materials were so brilliant and beautiful that it was hard to narrow down my selection. I picked out some fantastic fabrics, and she made me four outfits for summer wear. They cost $25.00 an outfit. Unbelievable. Full harem pants and coordinating blouses. Nothing was perfectly matched but rather color coordinated. What fun it was!

Our trip took us to the city of Varanasi, home of the Sarnath temple. I have always been fascinated with the Buddha, so I found the story of the stupa, a Buddhist religious monument found throughout India, to be particularly interesting. A stupa, originally a simple mound of mud or clay used to cover the supposed relics of the Buddha, is composed of five components. Each of these components—a square base, a hemispherical dome, a conical spire, a crescent moon, and a circular disc—is identified with one of the five cosmic elements, namely, earth, water, fire, air, and space, respectively. After the passing away of the Buddha, his remains were cremated and the ashes were divided and buried under stupas, which evolved into elaborate pagodas, which were then used as places of meditation.

Our next stop, another inch down the map, was Pakistan, where we settled in on a beautiful five-month-old houseboat. Everything was new. Local vendors would bring their shuttle boats and join us on the houseboat and try to sell us their goods, which could be fabrics, trinkets of all kinds, and things made of brass or wood. Trips to the city market filled my senses. We walked by walls of colorful spices that the local people would buy on the weekends. The smell was pungent and different from anything I had ever smelled, as their spices were all grown on the island.

The food served on the houseboat was delicious; however, we all got very sick. Evidently the dishes were not washed in sterilized water, and no matter how careful we all were, we were doomed. But we made the best of it and carried on with our journey.

Our next visit was to the mausoleum commissioned in 1632 by the Mughal emperor Shah Jahan to house the remains of his cherished wife. At the center of the mausoleum is the Taj Mahal. Built of shimmering white marble, it appears to change color depending on whether it is lit by sunlight or moonlight. It is important to know that when visiting the Taj Mahal, it must be seen at sunrise and sunset. I was so weak from the "turistas" I was still suffering from that I could barely stand. My doctor friend and his wife, George and Mae McAuley, literally carried me to the Taj in the early morning and in the evening. It was so very kind of them. The evening sunset hit the marble, turning it the most exquisite shade of orchid. I might never have seen the splendor of this magnificent mausoleum if they had not insisted on holding me under my arms, helping me walk. But they were determined that I not miss such a stunning symbol of India's rich history. It was a vision, an experience I shall never forget. Nor will I ever forget the kindness and determination of people I had only just met! It shouldn't be a surprise that Mae and George are still friends of mine to this day.

From then on, a great deal of our travel was along rough roads. We would be forced to stop while the peacocks with their shimmery turquoise bodies, bright plumes, and proud "I own the place" movements took their time crossing the bumpy dirt road to Pushkar, a town in the state of Rajasthan. It is one of the five sacred pilgrimage sites for devout Hindus. Every November, under the full moon, one of the largest camel fairs in the world becomes a destination for locals from miles around. In addition to the buying and selling of cattle, horses, and camels, it has become an important tourist attraction. Competitions such as one to determine the longest mustache, "matka phod," are huge attractions. More than three hundred thousand people and up to twenty thousand animals appear for this event. It was truly a spectacle. My friends and I were put up for the night in tents that were fenced in and guarded by police. At dinnertime we were entertained by fire eaters, dancers, and a lot of imaginative music. Gypsy music and snake charmers' flutes harmonized along with the animal cries and the tinkering of the sheep's bells. Full-moon fever had both locals and wide-eyed tourists in a frenzy of activity and celebration. It was unlike anything I have ever witnessed.

I would be remiss if I didn't mention that, for better or for worse, India is a true workout for the olfactory. My nose never knew so many scents were available. The fragrance of more than fifty thousand camels, cows, goats, and sheep permeated the air alongside every imaginable Indian spice and curry.

The next morning I awoke to see thousands of camels walking along the horizon, while the natives were sitting around in separate sections with all their gear. I had never seen so many animals in one place in my life. Nor would I ever again. But what really made the experience outstanding was that every village that had come to the fair was represented by a specific color. Looking toward the horizon was a feast of color for the eye. The tents, traditional costumes, and market stalls were a sea of exquisitely bright shades of red, blue, purple, orange, and yellow. This was the most unusual part of the trip, and it nourished my senses.

Our guide made sure that we did not miss the holy lake in the middle of this barren desert. This beautiful oasis, also held to be the holy lake of Pushkar, is said to have been formed when Lord Brahma wished to crush a demon on earth by dropping a lotus flower on him from the heavens. During the full moon of the Pushkar festival, the waters of the lake are magical. Anyone taking a dip in the lake water at dawn is entitled to a rite of passage: being absolved of sin.

Our group was set to travel to several more villages, but by that time I was pretty sick and Lalite had invited me to stay at his palatial home. I was reluctant because I did not know the ways of Indian men and was not 100 percent comfortable. But Lalite assured me that he would not be home. He had planned to journey to one of his other homes in the forest for a hunting trip. When I arrived in New Delhi and made my way to his home, there was a surprise waiting for me at the door: Lalite. My heart sank, but as I looked at him I realized his face was distorted. He had a very bad tooth problem, and his trip had to be canceled. He apologized as he saw the fear in my face, so I knew his intentions were honorable. I was just so ill that I had to stay. Lalite had his doctor come over to see me every morning and evening until I felt better. He also had two dozen fresh red roses brought to my room every day. I had never been treated in such a special way. Even Lalite's beautiful golden retriever stayed with me at my bedside at all times, watching over me. When I was back on my feet and wanted to get back to practicing my yoga, there was another surprise waiting for me. Lalite showed me to a beautiful ornate wrought-iron staircase that led up to a room with tatami wall covering. The lights in the room had brass shades with holes in them so when the light shone through, it danced gaily on the walls. It was a magical room that I shall never forget, and I began feeling much better now that I could practice yoga. I'm so glad I stayed because I enjoyed being Lalite's guest very much.

One of the evenings when I was feeling better, Lalite had guests for dinner. A very lovely couple, Rashmi and Francis Dore, were old friends of his who lived in Paris. We immediately liked one another, and the Dores became lifelong friends of mine. Rashmi created the most wonderful dinner parties, and there wasn't a time that I was in Paris that I did not see them. I was always entertained by them with fabulous dinner and great conversation. Rashmi is a grand hostess. She loves people, and they adore her. She is sophisticated, well educated, and seems to know everyone. She is also a sommelier, a wine-tasting specialist; this is an unusual position for a woman as most sommeliers are men. Francis was a liaison that represented the French arts to India. He belonged to the chamber of commerce in France and was also a professor—a well-informed Parisian, to say the least, and a very special man.

Many years later, as a guest of Lalite's, I joined Rashmi in India for her nephew's very special Hindu wedding. The reception was held at the home of the groom. His parents decorated the home with hundreds of marigolds, and the groom's stately white horse pranced around the yard with a special jeweled saddle that had been handed down from generation to generation. A boy about three years old sat behind him in the saddle, as a symbol of fertility. Then the groom and all the guests drove to a huge park. There were hundreds of people at the park, and I believe five different weddings were going on at the same time. There are only certain days of the year that are designated for marriage. The bride was waiting on a throne to see her groom ride up on a stately white horse. The groom wore a jeweled headpiece over his face. The traditional custom for an arranged marriage was for the bride to look out of the window and see this man, her husband-to-be, for the first time while he was still wearing the jeweled headdress. He dismounted and took a seat beside his bride on his designated throne.

It was such a special spectacle—very theatrical and emotional. The food and drink were wonderful, as was the music. The wedding activities went on for four more days (without me!). The brides in the Hindu religion do not wear white; instead, they wear beautiful, rich colors like emerald green, red, and brilliant blues. White is reserved for funerals.

There were many other customs and traditions that Lalite shared with me during my stay. Lalite had a tradition of his own, which I observed nightly. Every evening Lalite would put on his Nehru outfit and he would receive people who wanted to talk with him. They all seemed to want something: favors, jobs, school entry, merchandise, or money. I could see so clearly that they all had an agenda and wondered how Lalite was so tolerant. It was a family tradition.

The evening before I left India for America I was feeling much better, and Lalite asked me to join him for a dinner party. I realized previously that when he would enter a room, people swallowed him up, pushing me aside, so for this last evening I made a plan. Once everyone had arrived, I walked into the middle of the group of people who were already deep in conversation and introduced myself as Glorya from California, Lalite's guest. They welcomed me and soon dinner was served. I left them and went over to Lalite. Taking his arm, I sat down to eat dinner with him. It was a very foreign practice for me but it worked. Soon the hostess came over. She told Lalite that she thought he was wonderful because he had given up so much by taking over the leadership of the conglomerate left to him by his father. I asked Lalite how this worked for him and how he managed to handle all of it. Lalite told me, "I do not have an ax to grind, and I don't want anything from anyone." Later in my life when I pursued philanthropic endeavors I would come to be much more understanding of his stance.

I really enjoyed the magic and beauty of India. My journey enlightened me, and I feel I came home a spiritually stronger person. My strength was tested on this trip, and I passed with flying colors. There were so many things I dared to do that I never would have considered even a few years earlier, and certainly not while I was married to Don. When I returned home to the States, it took one complete year before I fully recovered from my illness. Despite this, India will always hold a special place in my heart as a mystical country. Many people wonder, *Why India? There is so much poverty.* Well, what I have learned is this: You find poverty in many parts of the world, but if you look for the beauty and the magic, you will most definitely find that, too.

I kept in touch with my host and friend Lalite Thaper until his death. Even though he attended USC, I wished he had been able to visit the United States again. I would have been thrilled and honored to have him as a guest at Amber Hills and to show him the magic of our wonderful country.

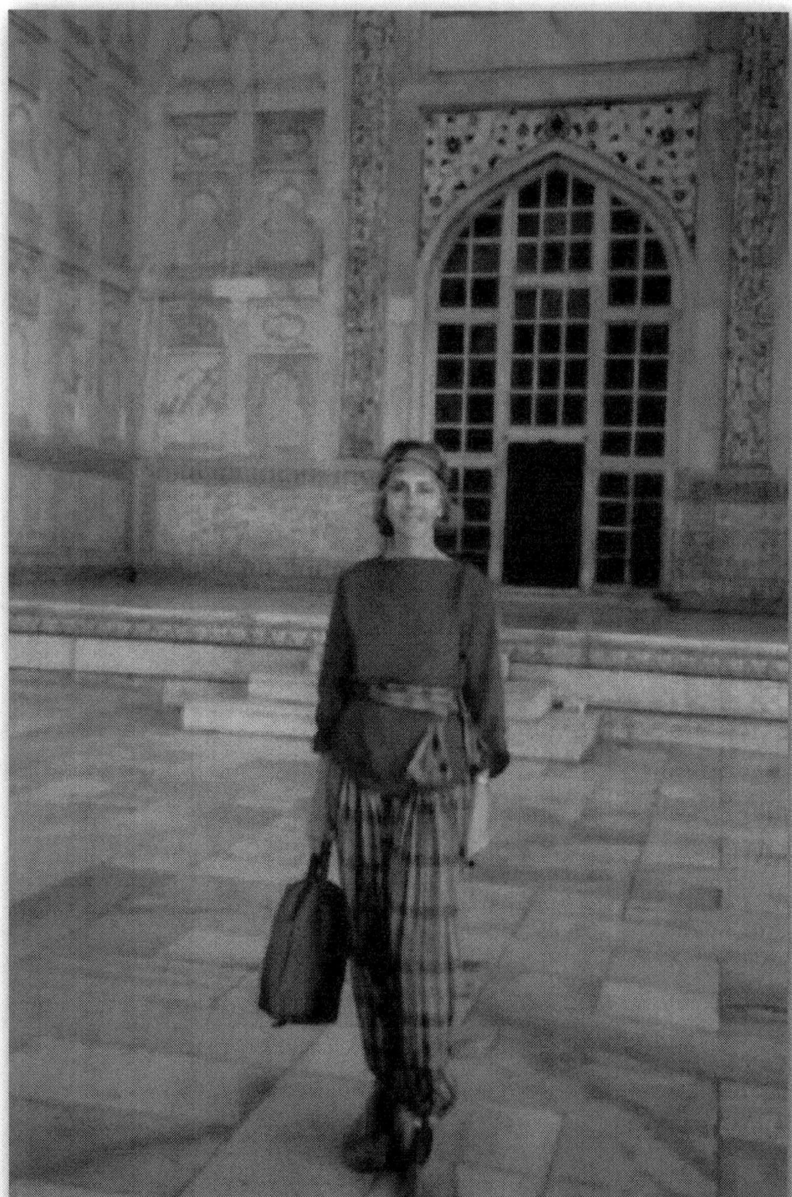

**Glorya in India**

# The Donald Bruce Kaufman Brentwood Branch Library

WHEN I RETURNED HOME FROM my trip, I threw myself back into working on the Donald Kaufman library, which I had been working on for several years. Because Don was a voracious reader, I thought a library would be a fitting memorial, and I was considering working on an addition to the 1,500-square-foot library on San Vicente in Brentwood. About six months after Don's death, I put in a call to the Brentwood Library and spoke with the librarian, Joan Baxter. I told her of my thoughts about building an addition and naming it after my late husband. Sometime later, Joan shared with me that when she hung up from our initial phone call, she told her staff, "I just spoke to a woman who is going to change our lives." Well, it was about to change my life, too. I had never done anything like this before. This would be my "testing of the waters" in the world of philanthropy, and my first step in the direction of bettering the lives of countless others.

My first step was a meeting with Councilman Marvin Braude. He assigned a deputy to show me many libraries throughout the city so that when it came time for me to choose an architect, I would know what worked best. The city librarian at the time, Wyman Jones, was also very helpful during this process. Finally, it was decided that a whole new library was needed. A 5,500-square-foot building was approved, and I hired and began work with Arthur Erickson, a very talented Canadian architect and a lovely man. He came up with a great design; however, it was rejected by the city council.

They felt it was too small and would be obsolete by the time the building was finished. They asked for an additional three thousand square feet. This was terrible news. Since the library was a public building, a fundraising campaign was started, and I would be matching the amount raised as a challenge grant. I was introduced to Mickey Bodek, who headed up the first fundraiser. She subsequently stepped down, and the Friends of the Library took over to raise the additional funds needed for the complete 8,500-square-foot design.

At about the same time, Arthur Erickson fell on hard times and declared bankruptcy. The construction temporarily came to a halt because of all the bills that had to be paid and the paperwork that had to be cleared up. It became a painful campaign because no one was really in charge. I filled the gap and stepped in again, adding another two thousand square feet to the library, bringing it to maximum capacity of 10,500 square feet. Paul Murdock, a young man employed by Arthur and just out of architectural school, took over. He designed the rest of the building and became instrumental in finishing the project. With the many delays, it took eleven years before the library opened its doors, but the end result is what was important: It became one of the city's most popular libraries.

When he first saw the space, Arthur immediately loved the big beautiful tree that belonged to the property next door. He designed a large window in the community room so that the tree became a focal point. He implemented a spherical design, which is best because it gives the librarian in the reception area the ability to easily keep an eye on the needs of all the visitors. It looked like a huge water tank to me, so Arthur went back to the drawing board and put the skylight on a tilt, and that made all the difference. My part in the design was to choose the interior colors and the furniture. I chose purple chairs and bannisters, off-white walls, and a beautiful greenish-blue tiling for the floors. Then, before he had to leave the project, Arthur designed a great room for the staff to have lunch and hang out in during their breaks, and a lovely community room, which is especially dear to my heart. It is named after my father, Samuel Pinkis. A very lifelike oil painting of my father hangs in the room.

I had commissioned a bust of Don for the library and had many meetings with the artist. Since it would be three-dimensional and in a place of prominence, I gave her many pictures of Don from every angle. When the bust was completed, the artist was thrilled with her work and could not wait to reveal it to me. Unfortunately, I was not so thrilled. It didn't look like him at all, but she was so happy I didn't have the heart to burst her bubble. The bust remained in the library until her death, and I then donated it to a Jewish home for the aged and commissioned a new bust with Donna Weiser. She did a fabulous likeness of Don that made me very happy. It sits on a pedestal on the main floor under a floating staircase.

It is fitting and of great comfort to me that my father be honored in the library with Don as they loved each other so much. I will always picture them playing snooker together. My dad died just two short years after Don, but he lived long enough for me to tell him that if it weren't for the love and support he gave me during my life, I don't know that I could have gotten past the loss of my husband. Knowing they watch over this library together gives me great comfort. The kindness of our patrons also gives me reason to feel proud. I have had strangers come up to me and tell me they would rather read in "my library" than at their own home. This tickles me so. The work on the library was a huge step in my healing process, and I was very proud of my accomplishment, as I know Don would have been so proud to be honored in this way. If that weren't enough cause to celebrate and be proud, the year the library was completed, the building design won the Los Angeles Business Council's $25^{th}$ Annual Urban Beautification Award. It gives me great solace that Don's library is not only an award-winning beauty, but one of the most highly used libraries in the city.

**Donald Bruce Kaufman Brentwood Branch Los Angeles Public Library**

**Left to right: John Kralick, librarian; Glorya; Arthur Ericsson, architect**

**The Kaufman family at the opening of the library**

Left to right: Donna Weiser, sculptor; Glorya Kaufman

Glorya accepting the Brentwood Chamber of Commerce's Citizen of the Year Award, 1985

# Accident in Italy

In May of 1994, seven of us, friends and family, rented a charming villa in Tuscany, near the west coast of Italy. We enjoyed many road trips to surrounding cities and interesting areas, and we took a train to Cinque Terre, an area in Northern Italy that had no roads. We went into a small bank next to the train station to exchange currency. As I came out of the bank with my friend, anesthesiologist Dr. Dona Warner, a motor scooter sped out of control, hitting me and Dona's uncle. Her uncle was uninjured, but I fell on my face and was unconscious for five to ten minutes.

I was driven by an ambulance to a nearby clinic which was closed, and then transported to an emergency facility in nearby Levanto where cuts over my right eyelid were sutured. The doctor did not want to administer anesthesia, but Dona insisted. X-rays of my head and chest were ordered, and cortisone was given. At Dona's urging I was transferred to the nearest major hospital, which was in La Spezia. In La Spezia other tests were performed, including blood tests, chest tests, an EKG, and a CAT scan. The list of injuries was long:

1. A mild cerebral concussion (no skull fracture)
2. Fracture of the lower third of the sternum (no underlying cardiac damage)
3. Subconjunctival hemorrhage, right eye (no retinal or corneal damage)
4. Skin lacerations on the right eyelid and right lip
5. 5Buccal mucosa laceration, left side

## Dona Warner: Friend and Physician

Glorya was treated with a tetanus shot, antibiotics, cortisone, and pain medication. The hospital at La Spezia was not as organized as those we are used to in America, but it was certainly adequate for her immediate needs, even though she was obliged to furnish her own toiletries. The nurse forgot her underarm temperature monitor many times and kept dropping and breaking them. Glorya shared her room with a lovely elderly lady who didn't speak English, whose family brought food that she generously shared with Glorya.

We visited her every morning to check on her condition and talk to the doctors. My daughter Lisa drove to La Spezia every evening to read to her as her facial injuries prevented her from doing so.

Glorya steadily improved, and after three days she was sitting up, totally alert, walking without dizziness, and eating with no nausea or vomiting. The swelling around her right eye was resolving, and she could open it enough to see. The doctor advised her to stay in the hospital for some more days in case of future complications, but Glorya wanted to go home.

Glorya's daughter Gayl flew in from Israel once she heard of the accident. She also wanted her mother to stay in Italy. Glorya and I discussed this and decided it would be best to be home in LA with a more advanced medical center to take care of any complications. Thus, all of us drove to Milan, where Glorya and I flew first class on Alitalia to LA, equipped with oxygen just in case she needed it. The rest of our group finished their vacation on beautiful Lake Maggiore, near Milan.

# The J. Ronald Reed Fiasco

DURING THE WORK ON THE library, I met a wonderful lady by the name of Betty Lasky. Betty was a member of the Friends of the Brentwood Library, and even though she was in her nineties, she still spoke beautifully at the library on the afternoon that we met. She told me all about her father, an American pioneer in motion-picture production, Jesse L. Lasky. He was a founder of Paramount Pictures with Adolph Zukor, and he had built a small museum, the Hollywood Heritage Museum, that she was having restored to preserve all of his memorabilia. The Hollywood Heritage Museum is famous for being previously known as the Lasky-DeMille Barn, where Hollywood's first feature film, Cecil B. DeMille's *The Squaw Man* was made.

I found Betty fascinating, and we both loved to dance. We made a date to meet downtown for an evening of dinner and dancing at the Biltmore Hotel. I brought a dance partner, and so did Betty. Her escort, J. Ronald Reed, was the man restoring her father's museum. Ron told me of his passion for restoration. One of his specialties was working with materials that brought back the art-deco period, a favorite of mine. His company, Restoration Studio, could reproduce anything in any medium, and he knew how to repair anything—or at least how to find the right workman to repair or make anything. He knew the best glass specialist, steel contractor, metalworker, and woodworker, all of them artists. Ron would pull everything together for his clients, delivering with great satisfaction anything the client could envision. In addition to being extremely talented, Ron was charming, and we soon became great friends. He had a son named Juan and bragged about him often. Juan Sequeira was from

Nicaragua, and there he and Ron, who also spoke Spanish, had an alligator farm and a factory that made ladies' handbags, belts, and shoes. Juan and Ron were partners in their Nicaraguan companies, Sweet Illusions and Salas. Ron seemed to have the Midas touch at whatever business he pursued.

Since Amber Hills was such a huge project for me, and Ron seemed knowledgeable about absolutely everything, I soon commissioned many artistic pieces for the grounds and the inside of my home.

Ron seemed to really listen to me, and he clearly understood my taste in art. He constructed a beautiful gate for the entrance to the estate according to my design, and he also made beautiful art-deco panels for inside the house. Together we designed my beautiful frosted glass door etched with two tango dancers and three bubble windows for the bathroom. I saw how terrific he was with people; he knew everyone. As I became more and more comfortable with him, I gave him the responsibility for hiring the gardeners, caring for the grounds, and spearheading the Amber Hills transformation project. I came to rely on Ron heavily. I had not had someone to rely on or help me make decisions since Don died. It felt good, and for the first time in a long time I was enjoying the company of a man, even though we were just friends. There was nothing romantic or physical about our relationship. We laughed a lot, which was new for me, and enjoyed creating special things for Amber Hills together. We would spend afternoons in and around LA in museums, and he was always elegant, polished, and articulate about all forms of art, from ancient to modern. This was new to me as well. Don never shared my passion for art. Quite simply, I enjoyed Ron's company tremendously.

Ron soon became my dance partner and traveling companion. We traveled together to Saint Petersburg, Paris, Barcelona, and Prague. We took tango lessons together and planned a dance trip to Argentina. We had great fun improving our tango techniques, dancing the nights away. We always had separate rooms and were both comfortable with this arrangement. He got along well with all my friends. Ron and I talked often about my children and my sadness at their absence from my life. In addition to being a companion and escort, he also became my confidant.

Ron gained my confidence over the seventeen years that we were friends. I could never have imagined that he was a con man. Unbeknown to me, Ron had been stealing from me for all those years by overcharging and double-charging, with all kinds of creative and manipulative paperwork. The word *embezzling* definitely comes to mind, and that is the word my accountant Harvey Bookstein used when he uncovered Ron's blatant thievery. When it all blew up in Ron's face (thanks to Harvey's help), I also found out from Enver and my assistant, Judy, that Juan was not Ron's son but his lover. I was humiliated, devastated, and felt like the biggest idiot imaginable. How could I have not seen all of this? How could I have been so stupid? Judy told me after the fact that she mistrusted him and felt he had ulterior motives, but she had had no proof. Other friends were afraid to speak up because they worried that I wouldn't believe them. I am very loyal and had known Ron for such a long time. I could not imagine someone taking advantage of my trust in this way. But what Harvey and I uncovered was criminal.

It was 2007, before I was onto Ron's con game, when things took a turn for the worse. He brought a woman named Carolyn B. Baker into my life under the guise of being the publicist that he insisted I needed. She was to help me put dance on the map—not just in Los Angeles, but around the world. At this point, after fifteen years of relying on Ron, who was I to question him? I thought I had outgrown my bad habit of leaning on a man without questioning his judgment, but here I was again, allowing someone else to do my thinking for me. I guess old habits really do die hard!

Carolyn was a very strong, loud woman. She convinced me that she knew everyone there was to know, and that she could help make my dreams come true. However, Carolyn was Ron's partner in crime, and the two of them had big plans for themselves, and for me. Of course, the plans they had for me were far less appealing. Their short-term goal was to scam me for as much money as they could. For instance, Carolyn would charge huge fees, insisting I hire a makeup artist for $500 to do my makeup for an event, but she would pocket a large portion of that fee. This type of scam, along with Ron overcharging for gardening, was small potatoes compared to their long-term goal.

My loyal assistant Judy, who was on to Ron, had recently moved to Maine. When she returned two years later, she was horrified at the important position and authority Ron now had in my life. She was determined to do whatever she could to save me from Ron and Carolyn's clutches. Their long-term goal, something that I did not even realize until after Ron was gone and Harvey, Judy, and I put the pieces together, was to have me committed as incompetent and take over my Glorya Kaufman Dance Foundation and its finances!

When Carolyn first came on board, I allowed her and Ron to talk me into changing my foundation into a corporate foundation, appointing Carolyn as secretary and Ron as treasurer. At this point in time, The Glorya Kaufman Dance Foundation had funded many dance organizations, programs, and the building of new schools, including UCLA's Kaufman Hall, the Juilliard School in New York, the Alvin Ailey Dance Foundation, Inner-City Arts, the Geffen Playhouse, and the Los Angeles Music Center. Without my knowledge, Ron and Carolyn employed Foundation Source, a company that handles foundation paperwork and taxes. I told them that I did not want anyone managing my foundation's accounts, but Carolyn said they were only having preliminary meetings. In fact, Ron and Carolyn had already hired Foundation Source against my wishes. This was their first step in setting me up to be declared mentally incompetent and stealing my foundation.

When I caught Carolyn doing things behind my back and confronted her, she became angry, telling me how much experience she had and that she knew what she was doing. She had a way of making up stories that were untrue about me, spreading them, and then taking credit for putting out the supposed fire. At one point she told me there was a rumor going around that I was broke and had no money left and that I needed her public-relations expertise to obliterate this story.

In March of 2009, I had a gala event in New York City for the opening of the Juilliard School. I told Carolyn that I did not need her to come on that trip. As I sat with my friend Deborah Schwartz on the plane, we looked over to see Carolyn right there with us in first class! She showed up at the hotel, at the event, and even elbowed her way into photographs. When I arrived in Paris with Deborah after the gala, my first order of business was to get

Carolyn off my payroll and out of my life. While I was in Paris, I wrote a letter dismissing her. We never had a written contract and dismissing her should have gone smoothly. But I couldn't seem to get rid of her.

In May of 2009, I intercepted a letter from Christine Meyers at Foundation Source to Carolyn and Ron that read in part:

> Dear Carolyn and Ron,
> I just wanted to take this opportunity to thank you for the wonderful dinner and company last night. I always think it makes a difference when you can put a face to a name. Apparently, the balance in the dance foundation account is 8 million dollars, so it looks like there was a significant transfer in from the Charitable Foundation. I'm e-mailing the documents to UBS today and I'll cc you both so you can see what needs to be signed.

Since Carolyn was no longer in my employ, it was plain from the letter that she and Ron were attempting to get control of the funds in my foundation. On June 19, I received a very disturbing letter from Andrew Bangser at Foundation Source. It read in part:

> We have a concern that Carolyn Baker has not acted in your best interest over these past few months, or in the best interest of your foundation. In the eight years of serving foundations we have had only one other similar situation where an Executive Director submitted expenses with personal benefit and told us not to speak to the donor, suggesting that the donor is no longer competent. That other situation turned out to be a case of fraud. Apparently Carolyn is working hard to keep you out of the loop. We wonder if you are aware that Carolyn and Ron Reed asked us to make them Directors of the Foundation, giving Ron and Carolyn two votes to your one and giving them the authority to remove you from the board. We did not do this; however, they have a document signed by you that appoints them as directors when you can no longer serve.

Carolyn and Ron must have slipped a document into a pile of papers for me to sign, and I had not noticed that it was a document appointing them as directors. When I gave a speech at a luncheon for City of Hope, Carolyn offered me a Xanax for my nerves. My friend Deborah later told me my speech was slow and my gaze glassy-eyed. I suspect that this was one of Carolyn's ploys to make me appear incompetent.

Ron and Carolyn were on their way to fulfilling their long-term goal of declaring me incompetent and taking over my foundation, attempting to outvote me and, with Ron as treasurer, helping themselves to $8 million! Because they had access to all my friends' names, telephone numbers, and addresses, they had contacted my friend Dee Dee in Washington, telling her I was losing my mind and needed a psychiatrist. Ron requested a referral for a doctor in Los Angeles from Dee Dee's husband, a well-known ob-gyn. Suddenly I understood why Dee Dee was calling me every day to check on how I was feeling.

Ron tried to scare my friend and assistant, Bobbie, telling her that I was not happy with her work and was going to fire her. Bobbie ignored his antagonistic remarks and said, "If Mrs. Kaufman doesn't like something, she will tell me herself." She did not like Ron and saw that he was trouble.

In June of 2009, my guesthouse was undergoing construction. I was unhappy with the sloppy work of the construction team and the fact that permits weren't in order as Ron had promised. I didn't like what I saw when I reviewed the paperwork for the project and it was reported to me that tools and machinery were missing. I let the construction workers go. Within a week I let the gardeners go as well. Ron was upset, voices were raised, and my faithful and protective Rhodesian ridgeback, Troy, was making a fuss in the house. Ron told me not to let him out, realizing Troy could attack him if he sensed I was threatened. That was it. Ron left. I never saw him again.

## Judy Reinhard: Friend and Assistant

My first encounter with Glorya was some years after the death of her husband, when she advertised for a part-time assistant. When we were first introduced at her accountant's office, I had no idea who she was or anything about her background. What I did know was that she was composed, confident, and calmly beautiful. I was accustomed to working in the male-dominated commercial world where no one was calm, serene, or beautiful. I explained that I was newly married and had just moved into a new home. What a surprise it was to discover that I lived within walking distance of her ranch home on Mandeville Canyon. There was never a moment of uneasiness between the two of us, and we worked well together. I grew to love her as a friend and became very protective of her. She was kind, loving, and so open that she just couldn't see when someone was out to use her. Between her husband's tragic death and the dismissive attitude of her children, I felt she had already had her share of trouble. Unfortunately, J. Ronald Reed proved to be the most destructive force in her life.

During the time Glorya was working on the library she was dedicating to her late husband, she was introduced to J. Ronald Reed, a charming, dapper, if not handsome, man who did what a con man does best. He gained Glorya's confidence, and she came to rely on him heavily. It would take Glorya's courage, her CPA, Harvey Bookstein, and me to expose him.

I left Glorya's employment for a few years, and when I returned, Ron was still there—in an even higher position of trust than he was in when I left! It was frightening to me. Glorya, still unaware of Ron's ulterior motives, was in the midst of setting up her dance foundation, and there was Ron in a position of authority. He had inserted a woman named Carolyn Baker as Glorya's publicist. She turned out to be nothing more than Ron's partner in crime, and she eventually stole Glorya's website. Along with Glorya's previous assistant, the three of them had funneled every possible cent into their own pockets. Between them they had Glorya surrounded. I was afraid they were moving in for the kill—literally. In the event of Glorya's demise, Ron would inherit the foundation. When I came across this paperwork, I wrote a letter stating that if anything happened to me or Glorya, the people at the bottom of it would be Ron Reed and his cohorts. In the letter I stated that there was paperwork incriminating Ron in his attempt to take over Glorya's dance foundation. In this paperwork, Ron also insinuated that Glorya was mentally incompetent. I sent the letter to Wil Roche, Glorya's attorney, and hid a copy for myself. It wasn't long afterward that Ron realized his days of stealing from Glorya were over.

I tried my best to collect evidence that he was embezzling. But he was clever and knew how to confuse things so that there were no cross-checks. I could only go on what was logical and what I knew to be true. First of all, Juan was not his son; he was his lover. I don't even know that Glorya realized Ron was gay. It certainly wasn't a stretch. Glorya's wonderful live-in groundskeeper and trusted friend, Enver, was onto Ron as well. Ron knew how protective Enver was of Glorya and hated that Enver was watching what he was doing on a daily basis. So when Glorya realized it was time for Enver to retire and bought him a home in Norwalk, Ron was thrilled on two scores: Enver would no longer be able to keep an eye on Ron, and, of course, Ron took a nice fee to "fix up" the house that Glorya bought for Enver, using the cheapest materials possible for the highest prices. I conferred with my son Scott, a contractor who finished the work on Glorya's duplex, and I suspected that Ron was spending Glorya's money on materials that were not for her.

When we finally got to the bottom of it all with our wonderful CPA Harvey Bookstein's help, we found some staggering discrepancies, but we still couldn't prove any of them! When it was decided to turn the guesthouse into a duplex, Ron's crew used cheap and illegal supplies from Mexico. They used lead on all the water connections, which would have gradually seeped into and contaminated the water supply.

I call her "Glory." After everything she has been through, she has remained strong and courageous in defeating those who wish to take advantage of her or do her harm. She is the kindest, gentlest person that there could ever be. She gives everyone the benefit of the doubt and second chances! She is a master at not only listening to but also understanding both sides of a story. Because of her beauty, kindness, and love of whimsy, many make the mistake of underestimating her. She is a formidable opponent in any situation. Glorya is an amazing businesswoman and extremely generous. It gives her incredible joy to be able to combine these two qualities and make a difference in the lives of others. I cherish our friendship and the many memories I carry in my heart.

# The Website Scam

I THOUGHT MY TROUBLES WERE over, but Carolyn Baker had set about yet another scam: She stole my website.

In the fall of 2009, after I had dismissed her as executive director of the Glorya Kaufman Dance Foundation, Carolyn B. Baker reregistered the domain names for my websites. She changed my passwords and usernames and locked me out.

In November of 2009 she sent me a letter stating that she would "provide the information" and restore the foundation's website for a payment of $30,220.

I appealed to the World Intellectual Property Organization (WIPO), arguing common-law trademark rights on the use of my name. According to the WIPO investigation, "Ms. Baker claimed intellectual property rights in the website and threatened to remove the website permanently, use it for other purposes, or sell it to the highest bidder."

On March 11, 2010, WIPO ruled that Ms. Baker had acted in bad faith, and ordered her to return the domain rights.

Meanwhile, I was pulled into small-claims court by Solters and Digney, a media-relations firm that had been engaged by Ms. Baker while she was my employee. They demanded payment for the remainder of the year. When our day in court arrived, the judge asked the principal what he planned to do for me for the rest of the year. When the man said, "Nothing," the judge laughed and said, "You are not entitled to get paid for nothing. Case dismissed!"

# Moving On

ONCE ALL THE LEGALITIES WERE taken care of and I had gotten Ron and Carolyn out of my life and my website back, I began to come down from the fight-or-flight mode I had been in for many months. I had trusted Ron and treated him as my confidant for seventeen years. I felt so stupid that I had not seen him for who he really was. I was beside myself and left for Paris to escape. The only trouble was that I could not escape from myself. I was horrified at my stupidity.

The weather in Paris was dreary, and I felt even drearier. My close friend Tae pointed out that I was out of sorts and that instead of being alone in Paris, I should be at a spa taking care of myself and being pampered. I decided she was right. I immediately made a reservation at the famous Golden Door in Escondido, California.

When I arrived at the Golden Door, I explained that I was not there for the popular reason, to lose weight. I was interested in stress management. That was arranged for me, and I took every class that dealt with stress. One afternoon, I spoke with one of the teachers, needing some sort of answer for how I could have been so blind, so stupid. The answer she offered me helped tremendously. She said, "How could you see? You cannot think in that way." My anxiety and my ability to forgive myself and heal was facilitated by her insight, along with a ritual that the Golden Door provides for its guests on the last day of the visit. There is a labyrinth on top of a hill for those who wish to participate in this healing ritual. At the end of the week, I wrote a note that was for my eyes only. Well, not exactly a note, more like two and a half pages of everything that was bothering me, angering me, and holding me back. When evening fell, a group of us dressed in Japanese robes with our notes clutched in our hands. One at a time, each of us followed the candlelit path to the labyrinth. Music played softly, and I could feel the breeze against my face as I circled a pail of fire. I had been instructed to put my letter of anger and disappointment into the pail of fire when I was ready, and to watch it go up in flames. All I could do was witness my anger and feelings of shame go up in a blaze. Heading back, I met up with a new friend, Diane Bigelow, who had just torched her letter. We walked back to our rooms together in silence. The last step in the healing ritual was to write a letter to myself about how I felt. The Golden Door would then hang onto my sealed letter, and after four months it would mail it to me. I felt more at peace than I had in a long time. Bad things happen to good people, and the good and the bad are the layers of one's life. After a lot of work, I decided to forgive myself for falling prey to a seventeen-year relationship built on lies and deceit. I was ready to move on again and follow my dreams. There would be no more looking back and judging myself, only looking ahead with excitement to the next adventure.

In June of 2014, J. Ron Reed died from septic shock.

## Wil Roche: Attorney

I first formally met Glorya at Amber Hills in May 2009 in connection with being considered to handle estate planning and other legal matters. Although I thought I'd never met Glorya, as I drove up the long drive that led to her residence, I couldn't help feeling that I'd been there before. When I got to the top of the drive and saw the lake in front of the house, I knew I had been there previously. Many years before, when I was working my way through law school as a housepainter for Paul Horst Painting, a prominent painting contractor in the area at the time, I had worked at Amber Hills. When I met Glorya a few minutes later, I asked her about Paul, whom she remembered vividly, and we talked about "old times." What a pleasant way to "meet" Glorya.

When I first began working with Glorya as an attorney, we had a lot to do and spent quite a bit of time together, almost always at Amber Hills. I was impressed by Glorya's artistic sensitivity, which was evident not only in how she had decorated her estate, both the residence and the grounds—the unique pieces of furniture, the unusual indoor and outdoor sculpture, the eclectic landscaping, and the bird refuge by the pond—but also in her own abstract paintings, which were hung in various places around the house. I liked their soothing colors and patterns very much.

Not long before I began working with Glorya, she had engaged Harvey A. Bookstein of RBZ, LLP as her CPA and financial advisor. In the course of going through Glorya's accounts, Harvey discovered that a longtime and trusted friend and travel companion of Glorya's, who oversaw all the construction and remodeling projects on the estate, had been taking serious financial advantage of her for quite some time. Learning this was a devastating blow to Glorya, who unfortunately had unquestioningly trusted her friend with these matters and had a difficult time believing he could have bilked her the way he did. At that time, there was also litigation pending with the trustees of her trusts over their failure to liquidate the large positions they held in AIG stock before it crashed during the economic downturn of 2008, which was very distressing to Glorya. There was also ongoing conflict between Glorya and her children over the disposition of Amber Hills, which Glorya wanted to sell and the children wanted to preserve so they could inherit it on Glorya's death. There were also issues with the person Glorya had hired to assist running her charitable foundation, who had her own ideas about how things should be done and did not seem very interested in carrying out Glorya's charitable wishes. All in all, it was an extremely tough time for Glorya.

At one particularly difficult point during this stressful period, Glorya had seemingly come to her wits' end. Needing a break, she decided to get away from it all and booked a week's stay at the Golden Door Spa in Escondido, California. When Glorya returned, I noticed right away that she had transformed herself and was ready to move on with her life in a new way, letting go of the old, toxic parts and welcoming the new, nourishing parts. It took her five or six years of hard work to make the transition into her new life, but Glorya stuck with it. Gradually, and successfully, she made a major transition. During this period, I was continually impressed by her internal strength and commitment and her willingness to make the changes necessary to grow, which is not an easy thing at any age and is particularly difficult later in life.

Something else that has always impressed me about Glorya is her passion for the arts, particularly dance, and her desire to share that passion with others, as well as her desire to help those who are less economically fortunate than she. Her numerous and extensive contributions to the furtherance of dance are legendary and don't need additional description here, but one thing that is worth mentioning in that regard is the tremendous and deeply moving impact her charitable gifts have made on those who have benefitted from them, which I've experienced firsthand.

One day, Glorya and I were visiting UCLA, where she had created and funded a dance facility in what had been the women's gym until the 1994 Northridge earthquake irreparably damaged it. A student, who knew Glorya was in the building because we had visited several classrooms where Glorya was introduced, came up to us and said, with tears in her eyes, "Mrs. Kaufman, I can't tell you how much what you have done means to me and how your gift has changed my life and made the fulfillment of my dreams possible. Thank you so very much." That was such a moving experience for all three of us, and I realized in that moment what a tremendous difference Glorya's gifts were making in people's lives.

Similarly, each year when I review the annual reports the Los Angeles Music Center provides Glorya relative to her "Glorya Kaufman Presents"–sponsored programs, I am also deeply touched by the good that her contributions have done and the people's lives she has positively affected. This applies not only to the world-class companies that come to perform in Los Angeles, but perhaps more importantly to the hundreds or by now thousands of children and others who but for Glorya's gifts would not get to see such performances or have the Music Center's outreach program brought to their schools.

In recent years, having done so much in the dance area, via Alvin Ailey, the Juilliard, UCLA Kaufman Hall, Glorya Kaufman Presents at the Music Center and the USC Kaufman School of Dance, and others, Glorya has begun directing her charitable-giving energies in other areas, particularly focusing on helping to make a positive difference in the lives of challenged individuals, including women and children. Over the past several years, we've periodically updated Glorya's charitable foundation to broaden its charitable purposes in line with her evolving perspective. I've seen and been touched by how deeply she cares about the causes she wants to support and the persons she wants to help, even though she doesn't know them individually, and by how much time and energy she puts into selecting the projects she wants to be involved in and the manner in which her gifts are structured so they produce the maximum benefit.

On a lighter note, one of the most fun things for me about knowing Glorya is receiving the e-mails she regularly sends out to friends, which range from political commentary to beautiful photos of nature and animals to touching stories demonstrating the best of human behavior to social issues to interesting "did-you-know?" facts and humor.

One of the most refreshing aspects of Glorya's personality is that in very important ways she has never lost touch with her roots and with the basic values she learned as a child. Despite her considerable wealth, in many respects Glorya continues to be the same girl from the Detroit area who could have grown up next door and been friends with any of us. Whenever we attend functions together, I can't help noticing that there are many persons who want to make contact with Glorya because they know who she is, even though they don't know her personally. I can see that they behold her as if she were on a pedestal. Thinking about that as I write this, I wish there were a way for me to somehow share with them the very human, kind, and interesting person Glorya is, who has struggles and disappointments, challenges and victories, just like all the rest of us.

In closing, I am thankful that life has given the privilege of wealth to someone like Glorya, who uses it for the greater good and will be remembered for doing so.

PART 4

# Philanthropy

# Putting My Best "Philanthropic" Foot Forward

My philanthropic drive comes from my Jewish heritage and my parents' influence. I feel extremely privileged to have the life that I have, with the ability and the means to make a difference in the lives of others. My great passion, of course, is dance. What I have observed is how incredibly important the arts are to higher education, emotional healing, and physical health. Every aspect of the human condition is affected. I have had the good fortune to meet many wonderful people who share this vision and have devoted their lives to working with children and adults by utilizing the tools of dance, art, music, and drama. I believe that the arts, as a form of communication that transcends the barriers of ethnicity, religion, language, or social status, can change the world.

With this idea in mind, I began to consider my first philanthropic endeavor devoted to dance. I had gotten my feet wet working on the Donald Bruce Kaufman Brentwood Branch Library. Now I took a deep dive into the complexities of strategic philanthropy. This would result in my work with UCLA, The Music Center, USC, and many other arts organizations.

## Anita Mann: Friend and Choreographer

There are certain people who come into your life, and you know that there is a greater purpose than just a casual encounter. Glorya Kaufman is one of those unique souls who was put on earth to make a difference. She doesn't just feed off the land, but rather she feeds the land, sowing the seeds that will grow and nurture the lucky ones who benefit from what she has planted. Dance is my love, career, and passion. Dance has given me more than I had ever dreamed it could. I am so proud of the art, and I thank Glorya for bringing the world of dance to so many to enjoy and admire this exciting form of entertainment. The future of dance is getting stronger as the Glorya Kaufman USC School of Dance will be educating and training some of the finest young dancers in our country.

## Vicki Simms: Psychologist and Philanthropist

My first introduction to Glorya was through mutual friends in the 1990s. I saw her as an artistic, colorful, and very bright lady. Several years after we met, I started a women's philanthropy group and asked Glorya to join; she was hesitant but became a very involved member. There were about seven woman in the group, and it was extremely helpful to share the ups and downs of our philanthropy decisions. It was in this group that Glorya and I got to know each other in a deeper and more personal way. I understood her family conflicts, as I had similar issues in my own family. Glorya and I were able to share our experiences in a very nonjudgmental manner and together we looked at how affluence and money had affected our family ties and connections.

As a psychotherapist I worked often with affluent families. I found that for some children of very successful parents, there were considerable difficulties in adequately separating from their parents and finding their own identities. These adult children never experienced or felt success from their own work efforts and instead developed false senses of identify through the wealth of their parents. This stifled their emotional growth and maturity and led to their sense of entitlement. Glorya was haunted by her children's entitlement issues. We further bonded as she came to grips with her inability to change these family dynamics and the fact that trying your best was not always good enough.

My personal experience of growing up in a challenging yet affluent family gave me an unusual understanding of Glorya's painful struggles. My life experience was different than Glorya's—I was the "rich child who did find my own identity"—but I watched the struggle of my older sibling who was unable to find her own identity and substituted it with demanding and destructive entitlements. Glorya and I often joked about writing a book about the issues of entitled children, as it was a topic that spoke to both of us.

I found it remarkable that after her husband's death and her children's abandonment of her, Glorya was able to maintain a sense of gratitude and generosity. She could have become a very angry and unhappy woman. I respected and admired her for finding a way to make her life happy and meaningful by sharing with others something that she so loved and enjoyed. Dance made her happy, and she is passing on many opportunities to others so that they can learn and enjoy the arts. How inspirational! In fact, I find her enthusiasm contagious.

This beautiful woman has so creatively found a way to give back. Glorya's work with USC is exemplary: She has created a transdisciplinary approach to dance that is transformative, and as such she has made a major and unique contribution. Who could have imagined putting together the arts and medicine?

To have Cedar Sinai Hospital attached to the dance program at USC Kaufman School of Dance is groundbreaking. She has put together ideas that have never been paired up before. Going against the grain this way was not only innovative but courageous, as she left herself open for criticism.

In the many years that I have known Glorya, she has always tried to be the best person that she could be. Whether successful or not, she has always moved forward with dignity. I bow to her. It takes great courage to stand up to an overbearing trust, to stand up to entitled and demanding children, to stand up to the powers that be at UCLA—and to live to tell about it!

From a psychologist's point of view, I believe that the average person would crumble under such pressure and resistance. Glorya remained true to her values, never willing to put them aside in any sort of desperation for relationships. She quite simply won't allow negativity in any form, whether it's from within or from without. Glorya and I shared stories of our difficult childhoods, realizing that our respective quests for perfection gave each of us the capacity to push forward under difficult circumstances and to value the gifts that we were given.

Glorya has often been treated as an "inheritor" of money when she should have been treated as a cocreator. She earned the wealth alongside her husband. In my mind they were a team of "original investors."

I learned from my father just how destructive money can be in families. He referred to money as being "a loaded gun." If not carefully used, it can destroy—and it did in Glorya's family. Glorya's loss of her husband and then her father was tragic enough, yet having to struggle over control of money just added one more tragedy to the lives of this entire family. Glorya's inability to be the matriarch of her own family because of a powerful special trustee made it impossible for her to be the steward of her own family estate, which has created a lifelong battle between her and her children.

This denial of Glorya's rights and of her authority became toxic to her relationship with her children and changed the family dynamics, possibly for generations. The special trustee's ability to usurp Glorya's power and role as the primary benefactor and trustee devalued her in every way. This dynamic elevated her children's feelings of entitlement and fed their narcissism. It is the job of all trustees to work with the benefactor to ensure not only the family's financial success, but equally and more importantly to ensure the continued stability of the family unit. This devaluation of Glorya kindled the children's disrespect of their mother as a provider and parent, damaging the entire family structure. This is a great loss—not just to Glorya but to her children and grandchildren.

I am extremely proud of my friend Glorya's diverse accomplishments. Dance is being recognized as a tool to support health programs for Alzheimer's, Parkinson's, and many forms of psychological and emotional ills. Her foundation supported that effort with programs such as Creating Health through Movement at the City of Hope. As a psychologist, I can say that this is truly just what the doctor ordered. To be able to help those less fortunate than yourself is a legacy that cannot be rivaled.

Glorya's legacy to her grandchildren and their children is not money or a plot of land. Her legacy is as a model of authenticity, of having the courage to face and overcome adversity and challenges, and of honing the ability to move forward, to be creative, and to give back to society so that others can benefit. Moving forward through the toughest of times with kindness is a legacy to be left behind for all the grandchildren and great-grandchildren to come so that they know this strength is in their genes. It is there to be tapped into when needed. This is what I pray her grandchildren and great-grandchildren have the opportunity to discover about their amazing grandmother.

This saying by Kristen Armstrong reminds me of my friend Glorya: "When we focus on our gratitude, the tide of disappointment goes out and the tide of love rushes in."

> Author's Note: Your understanding and support have been so very helpful to me. I treasure you and feel extremely fortunate to have you as a special friend in my life.

**Left to right: Anita Mann, Vicki Simms, Glorya Kaufman**

# Glorya Kaufman Hall

THE UCLA WOMEN'S GYM WAS built in 1930. When the 1994 earthquake hit, the iconic building suffered severe damage. Daniel Neuman was an acting dean at the time, and he knew that I loved dance. He took me on a tour of the beautiful but dilapidated building and asked me if I would be interested in rebuilding it into a wonderful dance facility. I decided to go with the plan and had my well-known and respected attorney, Ed Landry, write the contract. Unfortunately (and this is a good lesson for all philanthropists to keep in mind for their own gifts), the contract was written too broadly and did not specifically state that the building was to be exclusively used for dance—in fact, the word *dance* was nowhere in the contract. I had never attempted such a project and in my innocence did not question the terms.

The new Glorya Kaufman Hall was unveiled in 2004. Although the building was redesigned for dance, with seven sprung dance floors along with showers and every modern device to enhance dance programs, UCLA diverted its use to a department called World Arts and Culture. While dance classes were offered, UCLA does not have a BFA program in dance. This resulted in any class that did not have a classroom (ROTC, cooking classes, etc.) being held in the new building. I was very disappointed about UCLA's failure to create a dance program and house it in the beautiful hall that my gift intended to create. In 2010 I met Nigel Lythgoe when I was honored by the Dizzy Feet Foundation, which provides scholarships to teenage dancers. I showed him the UCLA building. He said, "Glorya, you need an advisory committee, and I will get one for you."

He did just that. The committee consisted of very well-known people in the dance and philanthropy world, such as Nigel, Rachel Moore (American Ballet CEO), Debbie Allen (dance school), Vicki Reynolds (three-time mayor of Beverly Hills), Paula Golden (now the president of the Broadcom Foundation), and other smart, illustrious individuals. We had two advisory meetings with Chancellor Gene Block and his faculty but were unable to convince them that dance was an essential curriculum or that dance was the sole reason for my gift to rebuild Kaufman Hall.

In frustration, I held off giving UCLA my last pledge payment for several years in hopes of a resolution. I finally gave up and decided that my friend Paula Golden was right when she said, "Glorya, it's time to find another school."

My final contract with UCLA states that my name is never to be removed from the building in case the time may come when my dreams for a rigorous dance school at UCLA are fulfilled. Dance has been proven to provide skills and discipline that make young people better students and improve their education. My hope is that one day UCLA will have an administration that understands the value of dance, not just as a source of entertainment but also as a source of cultural enrichment that can better students' minds and society.

Despite my deep disappointment in the way things worked out at UCLA, there are many causes dear to my heart, and I have been lucky to be able to direct my financial and personal resources to them. In 2008, I established The Glorya Kaufman Dance Foundation, a private foundation that provides funding and support to nonprofit organizations in the United States. Though I contribute to many projects, my foundation was initially grounded in my passion for dance as a changing force, but it is evolving to embrace many important causes that I choose to fund.

I believe that children are a gift and deserve to be treated as such. But they aren't all in a position to receive lovely benefits in life. That's where I wish to step in, as time and circumstances allow. They all deserve to experience the joy of dancing, regardless of race or financial background, and I am dedicated to making dance available to children as an invaluable tool for their development. I believe that dance can heal the mind, body, and spirit. I also believe that dance builds self-esteem and ignites creativity. I chose to help Covenant House, a wonderful organization dedicated to helping children get off the streets. I arranged for Dr. Dance in Santa Monica to provide dance classes at his dance studio for children who wanted to learn to dance. If even a handful of them are inspired enough by dance to turn their lives into something more, it will be worth it. If some of the children just enjoy the dancing so much that it enriches their lives, I feel rewarded. Yes, with a slight twist, my childhood dream of an orphanage could come true.

## Nigel Lythgoe: *American Idol* and *So You Think You Can Dance?*

I find Glorya Kaufman an exceptionally attractive woman. Her red hair and sparkling eyes provide an amazing insight into her wit and wisdom.

I first met this lovely lady in 2009, at the inaugural gala for the Dizzy Feet Foundation. Carrie Anne Inaba, a *Dancing with the Stars* judge, suggested that Glorya should receive the Dizzy Feet Foundation Impact Award for her contribution to dance. At this time I was unaware of Glorya's incredible philanthropic involvement in dance, which is, of course, my passion as well. After judiciously doing my homework, I found out that in Southern California dance is synonymous with the name Glorya Kaufman. The Dizzy Feet Foundation board was delighted to present Glorya with the Impact Award, which she gratefully agreed to accept. The event was an enormous success at the Dolby Theater at Hollywood and Highland. There was not an empty seat in the house. During a very entertaining evening of dance and comedy, Glorya received a large bouquet of flowers. Unfortunately, we didn't have an award to give to her due to a small mistake—we had forgotten to order one. Glorya is still waiting to receive her award, which has become somewhat of a running joke between the two of us.

The Dizzy Feet Foundation was formed to support, improve, and increase access to dance education in the United States. Knowing that Glorya had made incredible philanthropic contributions to dance, I wanted to know more about her and hopefully find a way of involving her in the foundation. Therefore, I invited her to lunch at Il Piccolino, one of my favorite luncheon restaurants on Robertson Boulevard, run by Silvio and Eddie of Le Dôme fame. My first impressions of Glorya were that she was smart, intelligent, shrewd, wary, frank, and honest. I didn't learn this from anything that was said directly to me but through general information I picked up during our conversation. I learned very quickly that Glorya does not take well to being asked for charitable contributions. Whatever donations she has made she made because she wanted to, not because she had been asked. She is independent in thought and does what she wants to do. Consequently, I have never asked for a donation for our foundation, nor will I. Her joy comes from being able to change kids' lives through providing them with the opportunities for growth and betterment. She certainly succeeds at her mission through her involvement with dance, literature, and various other art forms. Her donations to the Music Center, UCLA, Juilliard, Alvin Ailey, the Geffen Playhouse, USC, Inner-City Arts, and the Kaufman Brentwood Library put her on the map as the Duchess of Dance, a force to be admired.

At our first luncheon, Glorya and I got on so well that we became instant friends, bonding over our joint wish to change the world through dance. We both whined a little, bemoaning the fact that the arts are not part of the core curriculum in American schools. We also laughed a lot, put the world to rights, and genuinely enjoyed each other's company through our mutual love of dance. I have a most wonderful affinity with this woman. Her spirit, energy, humor, benevolence, joie de vivre, and vivacity lifts up my soul and reenergizes it. She knows what she can do for kids today to improve their lives tomorrow. I am blessed and proud to know her, to be her colleague, and more importantly to be her friend and kindred spirit.

## Paula Golden: Friend and Philanthropic Advisor

I first met Glorya Kaufman when she came in for a flu shot at Saint John's Health Center in Santa Monica, where I was vice president of the Saint John's Health Center Foundation. Glorya had served on the board previously but had never been a major donor to the hospital, having put her charitable endeavors into projects honoring her late husband or her passion for dance and the necessity for its exposure. Glorya and I struck up a conversation. In addition to her interest in the health center, I was immediately taken with her warm personality. Before I knew it, we were both wearing hard hats and I was giving her the grand tour of the construction site for the new health center, which was necessary due to the extensive damage the center suffered from the 1994 Northridge earthquake. Ever game, Glorya scampered along with me over beams and wires to take in the creation of the new campus. Moved by the vision for the new center, Glorya offered to make a generous gift to name the first-floor waiting room of the patient pavilion. Her primary concern was not that her name appear prominently but that the room be decorated with warm colors, comfortable chairs and sofas, a television, a convenient bathroom, good lighting for reading, and a coffee machine to accommodate the stressed family members who would be making use of the room for many long hours during their loved one's hospital stay.

With regard to the naming of Kaufman Hall, UCLA had truly failed a donor. I attended the last meeting with the chancellor that had been called by Glorya and her advisors—one of several they had called in a running conversation about the intended use of the Glorya Kaufman Hall—and I was appalled by the attitude of the chancellor and his academic team.

It was clear that UCLA had taken Glorya's money under the pretense of fulfilling her dream to create a premier school of dance at the university and had proceeded to write a pledge agreement that permitted them to make use of her gift without regard for these expressed wishes. The tin ear of the chancellor resulted in Glorya's disaffection and ultimately in her seeking out a more donor-sensitive university, the University of Southern California (USC), to create a school of dance. UCLA is the lesser for its failure to pay attention to a woman of substance, and USC is reaping worldwide accolades for the new school and conservatory that bear Glorya's name.

Author's note: Paula and I became friends in 1994. I was new at philanthropy, and her fundraising skills and experience working with large institutions were a great help. Paula knows what questions to ask and has written contracts and speeches for me out of the goodness of her heart. She is tireless and has always been there for me. I am extremely grateful for our friendship. I want to take this opportunity to tell her how much I appreciate her kindness and intelligence.

## Marilyn Fox: Artistic Director, Pacific Resident Theater

I first had the pleasure of meeting Glorya Kaufman at her Amber Hills home in Mandeville Canyon. One of my board members at Pacific Resident Theater, where I am the artistic director, took me there to enjoy an after-performance party celebrating Merce Cunningham and his dance company. They were performing at UCLA's Royce Hall, and Glorya was generously opening her beautiful home to them and passionately celebrating Merce's contribution to the art of dance.

I remember that I immediately had a positive impression of Glorya when I first saw her. She was beautiful, youthful, and filled with enthusiasm. It seemed like light emanated from her—as if a spotlight was softly following her, and she was basking in its glow. What a wonderful life-giving energy she had! And it was genuine. She seemed happy! How inspiring it was to observe. She seemed to know something that no one else knew. She appeared to be truly enjoying herself. She had the courage to be herself!

I was standing in Glorya's living room that night, looking at some beautiful pieces of colored glass that were on a table that had light under it. The glass pieces were illuminated, and I loved the way they looked. Glorya walked up to me and said, "Aren't they beautiful? They make me so happy!" I said, "I love them, too." We started to talk and ended up in Glorya's bedroom where she showed me some more of her objects of art. We had an immediate connection. She told me she loved dance and the arts, and I told her that I was an actress and ran a theater. She said she was an avid theatergoer and that she would love to come to Pacific Resident Theater and attend a performance.

It is now fifteen years later, and Glorya is still coming to PRT, where she has been a friend and supporter of our theater and my work as an actress all these years. She can always be counted on to be honest, enthusiastic, and wise in her support and comments. I have seen Glorya go through highs and lows during the time we have been friends. I have seen her weather disappointments on projects and in relationships. I have seen her have tremendous successes in her generous philanthropic work, whether it be promoting the art of dance, the art of theater, helping children, creating a library, or supporting hospitals.

What inspires and impresses me most about Glorya is her wonderfully positive attitude. She has undergone extreme losses in her life, but in spite of them she is dedicated to enjoying life and living it fully. She has a refreshing authenticity and healthy lack of self-criticism and guilt. What a wonderful inspiration to be around a woman who has the self-esteem to enjoy her life and live it freely, marching (dancing really!) to her own beat without fear or guilt. Without a doubt, Glorya has stayed so young and enthusiastic because of this wonderful ability she has to be true to herself.

Glorya is an Aquarian (I am, too), and her nature is humanitarian. She is often a loving guide to her friends, taking a great deal of time and care to help them to be true to themselves and help guide them to find their true calling. What a joy to it is to know this beautiful, inspiring, fun-loving, wise, and creative woman who has done so much for the arts in our city and continues to create her artistic legacy in Los Angeles for all of us to enjoy.

## Betsy Baytos: Friend, Dancer, and Choreographer

I was first introduced to Glorya Kaufman well before the mid-1990s, through a mutual colleague, Sue Weil. I had just begun researching eccentric dance for a documentary film and had yet to connect with anyone in the dance community or begin interviews. Sue thought that Glorya, with her love of dance, might make an interesting connection.

Although still living in New York, I was increasingly bicoastal when we met, and I instantly took a liking to her. What initially struck me was Glorya's accessibility, her insatiable childlike curiosity and infectious enthusiasm, her unpretentious and warm demeanor, and her obvious passion for dance. She was smart, she was real, and she cared. She understood my subject and immediately saw the potential, how big this project was, and how I could reconnect dance to its past and bring it into the future. Glorya was one of the very few who went out of her way to bring access to individuals to further help me in my quest. She believed in me, and that is the greatest gift anyone could ask for.

I have to admit I was in awe (I still am) when I first pulled up to her estate in Mandeville Canyon. As those large gates slowly opened, I was indeed a bit nervous. But then I saw a remarkable array of colorful, whimsical sculptures placed strategically along the winding drive, and I knew I had found a kindred spirit. Ever gracious, Glorya welcomed me warmly, and my eye was immediately drawn to the beautiful art-deco Erté pieces on display, as my costumes from my last Broadway show had been designed by the great artist himself. Casting a further glance, I noticed these large, wonderful paintings and was astonished to discover they were her creations, like the various home décor designs she had implemented throughout the house.

Seeing the Glorya Kaufman Hall at UCLA as a product of her vision, built around her explicit instruction, was yet another testament to her eye for beauty and detail. It was clear to me that Glorya was not just another patron but a truly gifted artist.

As I write this, I still can't believe how many dinners, gatherings, and introductions she has assembled on my behalf, to make others aware of my work. There were several letters of support to the Jerome Robbins Foundation, which assured my grant, and she invited me as part of her inner circle to dance events, galas, and concerts. The chance that Glorya would attend my premiere of *The Princess and the Frog* at the Walt Disney Studios was slim, but she knew how important this was to me, and, my God, she came and made sure people knew I had choreographed the film. When I traveled to London to research Frederic Ashton for my film, Glorya made a call to the Royal Ballet without hesitation. Completely soaked from a sudden rainstorm while visiting Paris, I splashed into her apartment for dinner with a French clown in tow; afterward we had the most delightful time sitting on the floor going through CDs.

But the most memorable moments spent with Glorya were simple: driving around after a New Year's dinner and gazing at Christmas lights or sitting around her kitchen counter sipping tea, talking about family, disappointments, and future dreams. I felt I had known her my entire life. She is a visionary and an extraordinary woman, but more than that, she is a mentor, a friend, and an inspiration. She is always there, and that's what keeps me going. And that is Glorya, an indomitable yet gentle, compassionate spirit. I know her dreams will be realized.

**Glorya at the UCLA gala for the opening of Glorya Kaufman Hall, 2004**

**Glorya receiving the Gold Medal from UCLA**

**Glorya with Nigel Lythgoe**

**Left to right: Betsy Baytos, Glorya, Merce Cunningham**

# Alvin Ailey, Inner-City Arts, and the Geffen Playhouse

## Alvin Ailey and Fordham University

I have tangoed in Santa Barbara, Buenos Aires, Paris, and at my own home in Los Angeles. Dance is such a profound part of my life, and I want with all my heart for it to become special to others. I decided to support The Alvin Ailey American Dance Theater by contributing generously to the Ailey School, which trains young people to become professional dancers, and by providing four scholarships a year for the Ailey program at Fordham University. My pledge provides resources for choreographers to produce new work. I was very excited about this because Alvin Ailey, who is credited with popularizing modern dance, has a special place in my heart. Being able to help create the innovative partnership between the Ailey School and Fordham University has left me truly happy. Fordham's bachelor of fine arts degree combines the finest in dance and liberal-arts education in a four-year program. The students complete a diverse curriculum while attending both institutions full-time, so they certainly have their work cut out for them. My grant includes a contribution to the Ailey Camp program. Every two years Ailey instructors come to Los Angeles to teach dance to our inner-city children.

### Judith Jamison: Former Artistic Director, Alvin Ailey American Dance Theater

Glorya's magnificent new gift symbolizes the importance of dance not only in Los Angeles but throughout the United States and the world. It will bring the Alvin Ailey American Dance Theater to center stage at the Music Center forever.

**Glorya with Judith Jamison and the Alvin Ailey inner-city kids**

## Inner-City Arts

Inner-City Arts, located in the heart of Skid Row in Los Angeles, is widely recognized as one of the nation's most effective arts-education providers. Cofounded in 1989 by Bob Bates and Irwin Jaeger, its arts programs for preschool to high-school children are a vital component in creating a safer, healthier Los Angeles. In 2009 I established the Glorya Kaufman Dance Academy to help children explore the world through movement. This grant, which will continue in perpetuity, provides some of the most underserved children in Los Angeles the opportunity to express themselves and experience the joy and healing power of dance.

Cynthia Harnish: Former President and CEO of Inner-City Arts

Inner-City Arts, with its commitment to at-risk children, has become an extraordinary oasis of peace, joy, and learning for the children of this city. Founded in 1989 in response to funding cuts that eliminated arts instruction from Los Angeles public schools, cofounders Bob Bates and Irwin Jaeger saw the need to offer at-risk children the opportunity to experience the power of creativity. The program offers opportunities for children to build artistic self-expression and learn to communicate feelings and ideas while seeing themselves as valuable, worthy, and capable of reaching their goals.

The intention of the Glorya Kaufman Dance Foundation gift to Inner-City Arts is to create a dance academy with a rich curriculum enabling teachers to give children the full benefit of dance. With this gift, sixteen thousand children will be able to participate in dance classes at no cost to them.

**Glorya with Inner-City Arts kids**

## The Geffen Playhouse

In 1994 the Westwood Playhouse was donated to UCLA with the understanding that Gilbert Cates, founder of the UCLA School of Theater, Film and Television would assume development. Cates renamed the theater the

Geffen Playhouse to honor entertainment mogul David Geffen for his generous founding gift. In 2001 the organization began a $17-million-dollar capital campaign to upgrade the theater. Gil was an amiable friend, and it was during this period that I joined the board and donated a patio to the redevelopment efforts. I was drawn to the Geffen's educational programs for underserved populations. Disadvantaged high-school students gain access to year-round opportunities to experience world-class live theater; interact with actors, directors, and other Geffen artists; and respond to their experiences through writing and theater workshops. The Geffen's Lights Up program partners with over forty nonprofit and social-service organizations. The program serves veterans, low-income seniors, at-risk youth, and homeless adults, giving them the opportunity to experience an entire season of live theater.

Regina Miller: Chief Development Officer, Geffen Playhouse
Glorya makes life beautiful for others.

I was lucky enough to meet Glorya when I started working at the Geffen Playhouse. I was the development director, with a passion for raising money and an even greater passion for creating deep-impact education programs in the community. Glorya made it clear to me from the start that her passion was grounded in giving inspiration and joy to the most underserved people in Los Angeles, whether they might be students, seniors, veterans, or frankly any others in need of some joy in their lives. She touched me with her belief that the arts were essential to the lifelong development of individuals and to the creation and sustenance of thriving communities.

Glorya has served on the Geffen board since 2004 and has greatly helped to inspire and create the beautiful Glorya Kaufman patio at the Geffen Playhouse. Many students, veterans, and senior groups enjoy our arts-engagement programs, which are held on her gorgeous patio year-round.

After many wonderful lunches, Glorya learned about my dance background. I shared with Glorya how, many years ago, I was on scholarship with Alvin Ailey, and an amazing woman named Denise Jefferson was my childhood hero. Glorya then joyfully laughed and remarked on what a small world it was, because she knew Denise and was going to be seeing her the following week! She recommended that I write to Denise and offered to hand-deliver the letter. I was deeply touched by Glorya's desire to reconnect me with Denise. This seemingly small favor truly meant the world to me, and I was able to express to Denise my gratitude for taking a chance on an overweight young girl who was passionate about dance many years ago! Thanks to Glorya's thoughtful spirit, two women were reconnected after many decades. This is particularly meaningful because a few months later, Denise passed away from cancer.

Glorya has an incredible heart, and I feel truly blessed to call her my friend. She enjoys every "little step she takes," and always does so with style and grace!

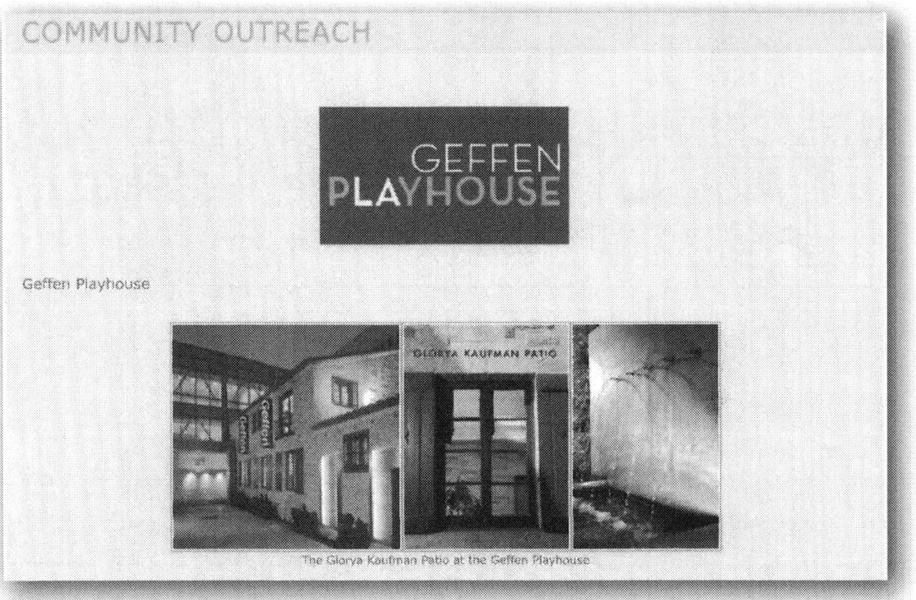


**Glorya Kaufman Patio at the Geffen Playhouse**

# Mar Vista Family Center and the Los Angeles Music Center

NEXT ON MY PHILANTHROPIC LIST was the Mar Vista Family Center in Culver City, California. Mar Vista was founded in 1977 as a preschool for low-income families and focused on engaging parents as partners in the education of their children. This special place, located in a high-risk neighborhood, offers a holistic approach to early-childhood education and peer mentorship. What touched me the most were the ex–gang members who now use their personal stories to help other youngsters avoid the same mistakes. I was very impressed by the dedication of the staff and board, the involvement of the community, and Mar Vista's amazing Lucia Diaz. The impact that this extraordinary woman has on gang intervention is changing the Mar Vista neighborhood. Lucia showed me an empty lot and said, "I want to build a youth center here, and I want it to open in 2008." Then, with a twinkle in her eye, she continued, "I love to dance, and I want a real dance floor for my kids." For me, that was it! I loved the idea. I donated a sprung floor to their facility to help encourage dance and movement activities.

The first dance performance I ever attended took place in my own living room, and the dancers were my parents. The future of dance in America is emerging from the shadows of the arts in our country. I have to say that dance is a much more sacred and revered art form in other countries. The tango is fine art in France and Argentina. I want the United States to catch up. I want to see that level of relevance in our country.

After the Juilliard Dance Ensemble presented four performances at UCLA's Kaufman Hall, I knew my next gift would be to the Juilliard School in New York to build a fabulous dance studio. It was indeed a privilege for me to help shape this beautiful new venue that shares my love of dance with the community. I am just so enamored with this eye-catching Glorya Kaufman Dance Studio, which faces Broadway. The architecture of this marvelous "looking-glass studio" brings the creativity of Juilliard students to the city so that passersby can be transported into the artistic realm, where, for a moment in time, they will become refreshed, inspired, and energized.

It was time to focus my attentions back at home in Los Angeles. In a down economy, the first casualty is the arts. The Los Angeles Music Center had almost no dance performances because they had no funding to bring in professional dancers, and they were literally ready to fold. I could not allow that to happen, so I decided to make a gift to the center, to allow it to continue to present internationally renowned dance companies, engage new audiences, and enhance outreach programs. Over 275 schools visit the Music Center annually to see rehearsals or programs.

I am thrilled that Glorya Kaufman Presents Dance at the Music Center can finally put dance and the spirit of dance into the proud place it deserves in the Los Angeles arts scene. The arts are critical to the lifeblood of the nation, and we must do our part to protect what could be lost. I am so proud to be able to bring world-class performances to our great city and to know that all summer long, classes are available to everyone on the patio of the Music Center.

In an attempt to catch my breath and have a giggle, I decided to do something fun and unusual. Partnering with the American Jewish University and being a huge fan of *Dancing with the Stars*, I presented *Dancing with the Rabbis*. My goal was just to get people dancing. For one magical evening, five of the most prominent area rabbis came together in the name of charity. Each one performed with a professional partner and was judged by the audience. The winner was Rabbi Zoe Klein, who turned out a stunning tango. Her award was a charitable donation to her favorite cause. The evening was full of energy and excitement, and I reached my goal: everyone danced and had a good time.

## Stephen Roundtree: President and CEO of the Music Center

The Music Center is an institution that has been built by strong women with vision, from Dorothy Chandler to Lillian Disney and Diane Disney Miller, Brindell Gottlieb, and now Glorya Kaufman, the single most important patron of dance in our time.

**Glorya at Mar Vista**

**Glorya and the former mayor of Los Angeles, Antonio Villaraigosa, at Mar Vista**

**Glorya dancing with the rabbis at American Jewish University**

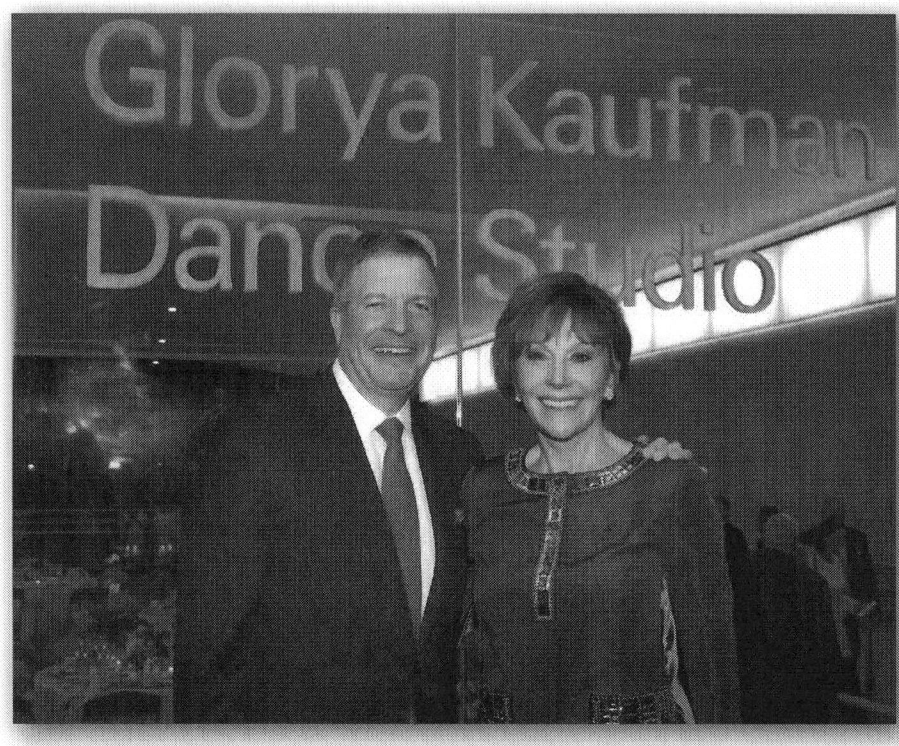


**Glorya with Joseph Polisi, president of Juilliard**

# The University of Southern California: A Dream Comes True

As 2012 approached I was to embark on the endeavor of my lifetime. I had dinner with Robert Cutietta, dean of the USC Thornton School of Music, and his lovely wife Marybeth at the University Club before attending a performance by Alonzo King LINES Ballet at the Bovard Auditorium. I asked Dean Cutietta why there was no dance program at USC. He replied that Marybeth was a dancer and that his daughter headed a dance company, so it was with all his heart that he wished there were a dance program at USC.

The two of us brainstormed, and the very next day Dean Cutietta met with President Max Nikias about the possibility of establishing a school of dance at the university. Within a week, Dean Cutietta invited me for lunch and presented me with a draft for a proposed dance school. After lunch, I took the dean for a tour of Kaufman Hall at UCLA. He was shocked to see that rehearsal rooms were empty, and there were no students running about in leotards.

For the most part, Kaufman Hall was being used as an annex for classes requiring extra space. Dean Cutietta promised me that a dance school at USC would not only be exclusively for dance, but it would be brimming over with dance students. For the first time, I could see the possibility of my dream becoming a reality.

The University of Southern California had been on a meteoric trajectory since Stephen B. Sample's ascendancy as the tenth president of the university in 1991. The vision and reach of USC, long maligned as the "University for Spoiled Children," changed overnight under his tenure. Sample and his successor, C. L. Max Nikias, have helped make it possible to envision a place on campus where the art of dance will be created, honed, and shaped. With Paula Golden's help and drawing on lessons I learned from my experience with UCLA, I structured a wonderful gift to create the USC Glorya Kaufman International Dance Center. Working closely with Dean Cutietta, and my old "posse" of advisors, we are forging a visionary institution at the university, one that is ready, willing, and able to embrace new ideas with energy and enthusiasm so that USC will take its place among leading dance venues in the world with premier professors, artists, and students.

For the first time I dared to believe that my vision, my dream, was about to be realized. The University of Southern California is one of the most beautiful campuses in the world, but it is also dedicated to providing students with a well-rounded education that will enable them to be a significant part of our future world. Our city's amazing renaissance is very exciting, and USC is at the hub of the city's rebirth. For many years I knew Los Angeles was lacking a home for dance, and I felt we needed a unique facility along with a world-class faculty committed to training young dance students to be performers and, more important, better "makers of dance." They will also learn business skills as well as how to interact with composers, choreographers, musicians, and songwriters.

The world-class faculty will be led by international choreographer William Forsythe. William has been active in the field of choreography for over forty-five years. He has reoriented the practice of ballet from classical repertoire to a dynamic twenty-first-century form. His principals and techniques have made him the most influential creator of his time. He has recently moved from Germany, where he had his own company for over twenty years, back to the United States to become Professor of Dance and Artistic Advisor at the University of Southern California Glorya Kaufman School of Dance. The students, faculty, staff, and (especially) I are ecstatic that William is joining our faculty. My dream of an innovative and exciting dance school is now in progress.

My trust in USC's ability to develop and execute my vision for a state-of-the-art dance building was well founded; our partnership turned out to be a dream come true. The Glorya Kaufman International Dance Center is a beautiful, gothic, brick building with a modern interior nestled among red crepe-myrtle trees and designed specifically to meet the needs of today's world of dance and dancers. The interior designs boast of beautiful appointments including a cluster of 1920 art-deco chandeliers at the entrance, which is a feast for the eyes. The marvelous huge windows let natural light pour into five rehearsal rooms, each named after a gem: Sapphire, Ruby, Turquoise, Amethyst, and Topaz. The physical beauty of the design by Pfeiffer Architects is exceptional. This building is designed especially for William Forsythe's "New Movement" in dance, a tribute to the innovative dance that will take place within its walls for years to come. My greatest hope is that the rest of the country will follow the lead of the USC/Kaufman Dance School.

## The Cedars-Sinai/USC Glorya Kaufman Dance Medicine Center

To extend the reach of innovation around dance, USC and Cedars Sinai decided to collaborate in opening up a center dedicated to dance athletes. I believe this will be the first such center in existence. They will be treating injuries and giving expert care to dancers while also conducting research on how to prevent common dance injuries.

The beauty of dance enriches and enhances our lives. Like any athlete, dancers rely on their sport to express and challenge themselves and their bodies. Scientists in the medical profession claim that dance helps to strengthen the immune system through muscular action. They have stepped up as champions of dance because they believe it mends and preserves the physical being and has proven to be a powerful "medicine" for such ailments as Alzheimer's, Parkinson's, and mental disorders. They insist that it reduces the risk of some cancers, and they claim that it benefits cardiovascular conditioning while promoting good health, including mobility and muscle coordination.

The Cedars-Sinai/USC Glorya Kaufman Dance Medicine Center is dedicated to educating professional student and amateur dancers on how to prevent and minimize dance-related injuries. An innovative partnership between Cedars-Sinai and the University of Southern California's Glorya Kaufman School of Dance, the center is led by Glenn Pfeffer, MD, a board-certified orthopaedic surgeon and director of the Foot and Ankle Program at the Cedars-Sinai Orthopaedic Center, and Margo Apostolos, PhD, an associate professor of Dance at the USC Glorya Kaufman School of Dance.

According to Dr. Apostolos:

> Most dancers intellectually understand the importance of doing stretching and warm-up exercises to prevent injuries so that they can continue practicing the art they love for many years to come. Unfortunately, many of them haven't received the best training about how to prevent injuries, or perhaps they've practiced those techniques incorrectly or inconsistently. Injuries can also occur when newcomers

> to dance are unfamiliar with the limits of their own bodies or those of their dance partners, or when experienced and professional dancers feel pressure to ignore minor problems until they become chronic or disabling. All of these situations create opportunities for team members from our collaborative Dance Medicine Center to step in and offer consultations, training, or corrective education to help keep dancers healthy and on their feet.

Medical Director Robert M. Bernstein, MD, at the Cedars-Sinai Orthopaedic Center, adds:

> Approximately eight years ago, Dr. Glenn Pfeffer, a foot and ankle surgeon from Cedar-Sinai with an interest in dance, and Dr. Margo Apostolos, a dance professor from USC, created a Dance Medicine Program within the Cedars-Sinai Orthopaedic Center. Upon the establishment of the USC Glorya Kaufman School of Dance, discussions ensued about connecting the two programs. I met with Glorya and members of the USC administration for lunch. Glorya and I immediately developed a deep friendship. The Dance Medicine Program subsequently remained the Cedar-Sinai/USC Glorya Kaufman Dance Medicine Program, incorporating many subspecialties, including foot and ankle surgery, sports-medicine pediatric orthopaedics, spine and trauma surgery, and physical therapy. The program has treated hundreds of professional, student, and amateur dancers, provided an annual medical conference for dancers, and established a research program focusing on both the treatment and prevention of dance injuries. It is led by an advisory board that includes some of the greatest names in dance and is chaired by Glorya herself.

### Robert Cutietta: Dean of the USC Thornton School of Music and the USC Glorya Kaufman School of Dance

The idea of starting a school of dance at the university erupted very abruptly.

I am dean of the Thornton School of Music at the University of Southern California and have been since 2002. As such I attend several concerts by our students and faculty every week.

There really were no dance events on campus since there was no dance degree, and finding time to attend off-campus events was often hard to do.

It was announced that Alonzo King LINES Ballet was coming to campus on November 7, 2011, to perform in Bovard Auditorium. My wife Marybeth and I decided we would attend. We invited the widower of a trustee to join us for dinner and the concert. He brought Glorya as his guest, and that is how we met.

We had a delightful time at dinner, and the conversation between the four of us was immediately natural, fun, and engaging. Somewhere during the dinner Glorya asked me why USC did not have a dance school. I replied that I really didn't know but had always lamented this. With the strong arts schools we already had in place, I explained, it was like we had a beautiful smile with a tooth missing. It wasn't like we had a bad tooth; there was just a gap where a tooth should be.

She asked what it would take to start a school. I had given this no thought at all, and I explained that it would be almost impossible since there had been no new schools formed at USC in decades, and it was unlikely that dance would be on the list for new schools that were needed.

She persisted. I explained that I really didn't know, but that schools had to be self-sustaining so the school would need an endowment and that it would need a building, teachers, and staff—everything. It would be overwhelming.

She persisted and said, "How much money would it take?" I had no idea whatsoever and said I would have to get back to her. She looked at me and said, "OK; let's look into it."

Now, remember that I knew this woman for less than an hour at this point. I learned later that she had researched me, had already thought about this, and had talked to her friend about it. He had assured her that I was "as good as my word" and she could completely trust me.

We went to the concert. I remember nothing about it. My mind was racing. I had no idea how the university would respond to this. I had no idea if it was possible. I had no idea if Glorya was serious.

After the concert we walked them to their car, and I said, "Glorya, were you serious?" She said, "Absolutely," and we arranged to have lunch to discuss it further.

It was late so I didn't want to bother the president of the university. Plus, I wanted to think this through a bit. The next morning, I called President Nikias and told him what had transpired; his response was, "Let's make it happen." I said to myself, *This is really exciting!*

At lunch Glorya was just as enthusiastic but clearly had no idea of what she was asking us to do. The thought of starting a school from scratch that would be a "major player" in the dance world was overwhelming to me. But we came to the general terms of the agreement at that lunch. The entire foundation of the deal took less than twenty-four hours from meeting to agreeing.

Glorya's friend, Paula Golden, president of the Broadcom Foundation, wrote the contract. It took about ten months of negotiation to work out the deal. USC was very happy with the final proposal.

This dinner started an amazing journey, a journey I had not anticipated—one I could not have imagined in my wildest imagination.

One of the first things Glorya told me was that she wanted me to meet "an amazing dancer and woman." This worried me because it was clear she hoped this person would help design the dance school. I had no idea what to expect. What would happen if I didn't like this person? What if we disagreed artistically on the future direction of the school? What if this person had no interest in helping?

That person was Jodie Gates. Glorya and I drove down to Orange County to meet her, and immediately my concerns were gone. Jodie was the perfect artist/teacher to help, and we instantly struck up a good working relationship. From there, creating the school became a journey that would last many years.

Everyone seemed to have an opinion on what we should do. For example, I remember receiving one passionate e-mail saying we should be the first school to offer a degree in ballroom dancing. Others insisted that, as we were located in Los Angeles, we should only do commercial dance. Still others said we should become the "West Coast version" of some other school.

None of these suggestions made any sense to me. We needed a true reason to exist and move forward. A turning point came when Glorya, Jodie, and I traveled to Frankfurt, Germany, to meet William Forsythe. We went to pick his brain, but after just a few hours with him, the three of us wanted him as part of our team.

After our first dinner with Bill, I went back to my room and wrote up an offer for him to join our faculty. I know this was bold, but it seemed quite natural. The next day Jodie and I presented it to him, and he was shocked.

I think Bill was honored to be asked, but it was so different from what any of us were thinking just hours earlier that it took awhile for it all to sink in. We stayed for another day, and by the time we left, I think we were all warmed up to the idea. I feel there was a major shift in our thinking during that visit. Prior to it we were asking, "What should we do?" After our conversations with Bill, the question became much more "What is needed in the dance field?" This subtle but important change made all the difference.

When we asked the question this way, it was pretty clear that the dance field needed a whole new generation of dancers who viewed themselves as artists who create dance. This was a very different way for us to look at the field and is what eventually undergirded the curriculum we created.

During this time we had much more to do than just create the curriculum (a major undertaking in itself). We also had to hire an entire staff and faculty and to design and build a building. For me, this was all in addition to the job I already had as dean of the Thornton School. Thank God for Jodie and two other staff members from Thornton, Jeff Decaen and Susan Lopez, who worked with us, tirelessly, to create this new school.

The university provided us with a wonderful location for the building. President Nikias had the entire say on the outside look of the building with the exception of the surrounding trees, which he allowed Glorya to choose. Glorya had the final say on the interior design of the building.

We started the process of interviewing architects and going to visit other dance facilities around the country. From this, a building started to evolve. What was great was that we could design the building to accommodate the actual curriculum that was now coming into focus. Jodie had conceived of a novel but demanding approach to the curriculum. This design mandated certain types of spaces and dance studios. We could design these into our blueprints and end up with a building that perfectly matched its function.

So that is how the school came about. It took four years from the time Glorya and I met until we actually had students walk into our new school. For the first year, the school was housed in temporary facilities, as it would be another year until the building was finished.

## Jodie Gates: Vice Dean and Director of the USC Glorya Kaufman School of Dance

With great joy, my life has been dedicated to the field of dance. As a teenager in Northern California, I was discovered by the revolutionary leader in contemporary ballet, Robert Joffrey, the founder and director of the Joffrey Ballet. At sixteen years old, I moved to New York City to join the Joffrey Ballet. I have always been a very hard worker with a pioneering and tenacious spirit and most certainly a perfectionist. The most important theme throughout my life has been sharing my love for dance through performing, directing, choreographing, and teaching. Dance as a profession has given me valuable and transferable skills that have shaped who I am today.

I have always had a pioneering spirit, have flourished at facilitating projects, and have enjoyed teaching students and professionals since I was in my early twenties. In 2005, I moved to Southern California and settled in Laguna Beach, where I founded the Laguna Dance Festival, a nonprofit organization dedicated to dance education and presentation.

From 2006 to 2011, the name "Glorya Kaufman" kept coming up. A friend, Ariane MacDonald, who is affiliated with the MacDonald Galleries in Laguna Beach, told me I simply must meet Glorya Kaufman. Almost immediately after Ariane's suggestion, Jane Jelenko, who was the president of Center Dance Arts at the Music Center, also declared that I must meet her friend Glorya Kaufman, and she brought her to see what I was teaching the students at UC–Irvine. Finally, circa 2011, an extraordinary artist by the name of Desmond Richardson told me he was having dinner with Glorya Kaufman; he asked if I wanted to join them. Did I ever! I had to meet this woman. Well, we hit it off and bonded over our mutual appreciation and shared passion for dance as a force for change. It wasn't long before we were attending dance performances and other special events together. She came to see my curated performances at the Laguna Dance Festival along with my choreography and collaborative projects at UC–Irvine. First and foremost, I have a great respect and admiration for what she has accomplished and her prolific work on behalf of dance. It is rewarding to see not only how happy dance has made her but also the extent to which she has transformed the profession. Glorya is truly looking to not just develop and nurture young, talented dancers but also innovators and entrepreneurs, leaders in the field, people who can make a difference in the creation of new art forms and new jobs that will secure work for the next generation. It's so encouraging to see her real desire to help the community by helping individuals. She's way ahead of her time.

One day Glorya shared with me her thoughts of giving a gift to USC. She was well known for her many contributions to other prestigious dance schools and programs. I thought it would be a great fit. She asked me if I would be interested in consulting with USC in building a curriculum. I was overjoyed and considered this the opportunity of a lifetime, but I also knew it was a monumental task. Rob and I designed the curriculum and the BFA program together; I also sought advice from and consulted with the dance experts in my international network. At USC, we reimagined dance education for today's world; we call it "the New Movement."

As my work with Rob and Glorya took off, I told them that there was someone they absolutely had to meet: my dear friend William Forsythe, who is also an educator, visual artist, and prolific choreographer. Soon after our trip to Frankfurt, Germany, Bill came to visit campus, and we began brainstorming ideas and possibilities. His ideas flow endlessly, and he continues to inspire all who meet him. As he shifted his focus back to the United States and to his desire to teach his methodologies at USC Kaufman, Bill agreed to be a part of building the legacy. He is now a professor on faculty and artistic advisor of the newly launched USC Choreographic Institute. This was such a gift to all of us, as his teachings and wisdom run deep, and his advice is boundless. Soon after, we hired a stellar group of faculty members who carry forth the vision and teach students in a new way that honors tradition yet pushes the boundaries—a group of educators who are all respected in the field on their own merits and are not afraid to be risk-takers with regard to creating a New Movement model for dance in higher education.

The students, faculty, staff, and really all of us know this is a special time and a rare chance to make many wonderful "firsts" by contributing to the field with a new approach to dance education, building a healthy culture, and developing hybrid dancers who will be leaders in the field.

As our first year with the dance majors closes and the new academic year opens with our move into a new building, we look ahead with excitement. We saw our first class of BFA students thrive, and our second class is ready to storm into the doors. We have over 1100 nonmajors enrolled, and our seventy minors will develop an appreciation for the profession and art form. I can only say that we have exceeded our dreams. We have had an opportunity to have so many "firsts," and the list keeps growing. The students were selected from a competitive applicant pool, and while they are very talented, bright, and earnest, they are still curious and innocent. Quite simply, they are magic. The legacy Glorya launched by creating an opportunity for other patrons to support a pioneering vision for dance at California's oldest private research university is one I am so very proud to be a part of. I am so thankful to Glorya for her vision and her determination. But mostly I am grateful for her friendship, which I hold so dearly in my heart.

### William Forsythe: Professor of Dance and Artistic Advisor, USC Glorya Kaufman School of Dance

Glorya Kaufman has an absolutely uninhibited love for dance and dancers. She has found dance to be an endless source of joy in her life and her enthusiasm for the art form knows no bounds. For decades she has translated this love into an unselfish generosity that has had and will continue to have a benevolent effect on generations of dancers and dance-makers. Through her vision and actions, she has set a truly exceptional standard for what the support of an artistic practice can be. I would like to say, finally, that of all of Glorya's gifts come through her great big heart.

**Breaking ground at USC**

**Left to right: Dean Rob Cutietta, Glorya Kaufman, Marybeth Cutietta**

**USC President Max Nikias with Glorya Kaufman**

# The Dance Continues

It takes a very long time to become young.

—Pablo Picasso

Today I feel younger and more alive than I have in many years. Writing this book has been a fabulous journey for me. It has allowed me to process the many influences, good and bad, that have made me a stronger, better person. And most important, it enabled me to reflect on the great friends I have and how much they have contributed to my life. For them, I will continue to strive to be the best I can be.

Life is full of surprises, twists, turns, and kicks. I spent much of my married life working to fulfill my college degree. Wherever Don and I lived, I found the nearest college and took classes toward my degree. I attended college in Detroit, Arizona, and UC–Irvine and UCLA in California, but I never fulfilled enough credits to obtain my degree. Today, I hold three honorary degrees: In 2010, I received the title of Honorary Doctor of Humane Letters from the Juilliard School. I received an honorary doctorate from Fordham University in 2011 and an honorary doctorate from USC in 2013. I also received a gold medal from UCLA.

I have mentioned my dream of founding an orphanage throughout this book. This year will bring me one step closer to fulfilling that dream. We are moving forward with plans to refurbish a building at Vista Del Mar in Los

Angeles. Vista Del Mar was originally incorporated in 1908 as the Jewish Orphans Home of Southern California, and it served the growing population of Jewish children living in the streets. Today, Vista Del Mar serves the community by offering high-quality treatment programs for children with significant emotional, social, learning, and developmental disabilities. We will be building a three-hundred-seat theater for students, with rehearsal rooms and dressing rooms. The redesigned building will allow children to participate in movement, dance, and dance therapy classes, and the theater will be available for use by the local arts community. We know from research studies that the combination of music and dance can help the brain reorganize itself. The implications of this research are particularly exciting for children who have experienced trauma or who have faced developmental challenges. I am very fortunate to be in a position to make a difference in these children's lives. Today, Vista Del Mar still places orphaned children in good homes. My childhood dream has come true.

My life has been more than I ever hoped for, and I would love for my legacy to be one of hope for others. My dance card is not full yet. There is still some space available, and I plan to fill it with some surprises. I have a few more tzedakah boxes to fill. With the marionette strings severed, I am free from constraint and plan to dance many more, lovely dances before I hang up my dancing shoes. As I did as a teenager back in Detroit, as long as I have the strength and will to do so, I will leave no dance undanced!

I would like to close with a quote that is attributed to Chinese philosopher Chuang Tzu: "Just when the caterpillar thought the world was over, it became a butterfly."

# Acknowledgments

I DECIDED TO WRITE THIS book after much coaxing from friends, especially from Luan Phan, who promised me he would help me with whatever he could. He did just that.

It is difficult for me to talk about myself, and I want to thank the many loving and caring friends and colleagues who have been kind enough to add their thoughts and memories to this manuscript. Thank you, Paula Golden, Wil Roche, Harvey Bookstein, Sue Lapin, Tae Hee Danos, Jodie Gates, Robert Cutietta, William Forsythe, Nigel Lythgoe, Marilyn Fox, Vicki Simms, Regina Miller, Bobbie Homari, Enver White, Reza Neghabat, Margaret Pace, Norris Bishton, Harriette Craig-Neghabat, Betsy Baytos, Elizabeth Juen Waltz, Joseph Dyrcz, Dona Warner, Cynthia Harnish, Anita Mann, and Judy Reinhard.

Many thanks to my editors, Paula Golden, Eric Jensen, and Luan Phan. Thanks to Richard Thompson for capturing all the wonderful photos in the book. Stephanie Klienman took my concept for the front cover and made it come alive, and Michele Mattei contributed the very special image on the back cover.

I asked Deborah Schwartz to collaborate with me in writing the book. I have known her since 1969, and we have a very special connection with each other. She did a wonderful job helping me tell this story. I am grateful for her sensitivity and love. Thank you, Debbie.

Very special thanks to Max Nikias, president of the University of Southern California. If it weren't for you there would be no USC School of Dance. Thank you for saying yes, Max!

# About the Authors

GLORYA KAUFMAN IS A LOS Angeles–based philanthropist and founder of the Glorya Kaufman Dance Foundation.

Published author Deborah Schwartz produced and wrote over fifty episodes of the globally popular television show *Baywatch* and the hit inspirational film *Soul Surfer*.

39244330R00131

Made in the USA
San Bernardino, CA
21 September 2016